BIBL SECRETS TO HEAL YOUR BODY & SOUL

Cover design: Rejenne Pavone

ISBN: 9798521317257

BIBLICAL SECRETS TO HEAL YOUR BODY & SOUL

DISCOVER HOW ANCIENT WISDOM & THE NEWEST RESEARCH CAN HELP YOU FEEL BETTER FAST

Kathleen Hampton

CHRISTIAN BIOHACKING:
THE BEST OF SCIENCE & THE BIBLE

Dedication

To Mom,

one of my first biohacking students:

Thank you for your love and encouragement

from the great cloud of witnesses in heaven.

Your eagerness to learn still inspires me.

Foreword

Every once in a while, a book comes along that's truly revolutionary. Such is the case with *Biblical Secrets to Heal Your Body and Soul*.

And like all revolutionaries before her, Kathleen Hampton has paid a high price for her bold insights. She's been accused of "New Age sympathies." The medical community thinks she's too spiritual; Christians think she's too scientific.

But the truth – *as you'll soon discover* – is that God has perfectly fashioned a vessel to carry fresh revelation to the Body of Christ. On these pages, she truly brings together the best of science and the Bible, based on a lifetime of in-depth study in both fields.

Kathleen courageously points the church back to what the Bible *actually says* about health and healing, rather than rehashing manmade traditions born more of despair than faith.

But even while she harkens back to the ancient wisdom of God's Word – and the church fathers – she leaps forward into the high-tech future alongside the brightest minds in modern medicine.

The result is a rare gem of a book that–*for those who have ears to hear* and the determination to implement what they discover–has the power to radically transform our approach to physical well-being.

But what I found most extraordinary is the way Kathleen makes the case that, before we can change our approach to health, we must first change the way we approach God in worship.

It sounds cliché, but I literally couldn't put this book down. If you approach it with an open heart, I suspect you'll have the same experience.

Blessings,

Donna Partow
Best-selling author, *Becoming the Woman I Want to Be: A 90-Day Journey to Renewing Spirit, Soul & Body*

A Gift for You

You are holding in your hands a powerful book. What better way to get started than with a powerful tool to get your healings flowing even faster?

So I'd like to give you a gift, the *Biblical Secrets to Heal Your Body & Soul Companion Workbook.* This workbook contains every activation in the book, checklists, and space to personalize scriptures, prayers, and record your healing miracles—everything you need to focus your efforts to feel better fast.

I am certain this free resource will be a blessing to you. Please visit gift.TheHighPraise.com to get your free copy.

Robust health to you,
Kathleen Hampton

CONTENTS

Biblical Secrets
to
Heal Your Body & Soul

Introduction

I n 2004, I was forty-six years old and I had 9-year-old twins at home. My hair fell out in clumps, I weighed less than a hundred pounds, and loose flesh hung from my bones. I entered early menopause and was rapidly losing my eyesight. I had holes in my liver, diverticulitis, osteoporosis, arthritis, gall bladder disease, narcolepsy, severe insomnia, adult ADHD, hypothyroidism, frequent neck spasms, and adrenal fatigue.

The doctors couldn't figure out why all of this was happening to me; they could only prescribe medication to relieve some of the symptoms. Everything hurt and I was sure my kids would grow up without their mother.

Natural treatments, remedies, and lifestyle changes based on the latest research—*sometimes they are called "biohacks"*—only got me so far. I was desperate for miracles. So I turned to the Lord, who showed me ancient wisdom in the Word. Among the most important biblical strategies I discovered was "high praise." Throughout this book, I'm going to show you what it is, what it does, and how to combine it with the best science-based biohacks.

(NOTE: You will learn all about high praise in Chapter 3. For now, here is a quick definition: "Exaltation that is focused entirely on God with no mention of the person who is praising or any temporary earthly circumstances.")

Most of us already combine natural treatments with prayer. But the high praise in Psalm 149 is like prayer on steroids. I had already been praying ("God help me PLEASE!") but was still on the edge of death.

So I started combining the natural healing biohacks with what the Bible said about healing. I studied and obeyed every scripture I felt the Holy Spirit was highlighting.

For example, I learned from the natural biohackers how important breathing was to trigger the body into the resting mode. Then by "coincidence" (thank You, Holy Spirit!) I came across several verses in my Bible about rest, such as *"Let us therefore be diligent to enter that rest"* (Heb. 4:11a NKJV). Next, I set my mind to learn how to enter that rest and stay there for longer and longer periods of time.

Once I took that first step, the Lord showed me one biblical biohack after another. The more I learned from the Bible—while also utilizing the natural science available—the faster the healings came. God healed one disease after another and my kids got their mom back.

I define "Christian biohacking" or "biblical biohacking" as "the best of science and the Bible." It's the combination of the newest research and the ancient wisdom of scripture, working together to help you feel better fast. You will learn all about this exciting "technology" in Chapter 3.

Now in my sixties, I have more energy, stamina, health, intellectual capacity, and creativity than I had in my twenties and thirties. I am off all those prescription drugs I took every day.

God truly renewed my youth like the eagle's (Ps. 103:5). There are many promises for health and vitality in the Word. Here is another: *"With long life I will satisfy him, and show him My salvation [deliverance, welfare, prosperity, victory]"* (Ps. 91:16).

We don't know why everyone isn't healed. But God's promises for a robust life were fulfilled for me. Now I'm on a mission to teach these biblical biohacks to as many people as I can so that we become a stronger, more powerful, and winsome church. It is my prayer that you power up with this beautiful gift from God and learn even more about how to bring healing and health to the body of Christ.

This Book Is For You If…

Do you want the long, vibrant, health-filled life promised in Psalm 91? Do you have low energy, a foggy brain, or a nagging health issue that will not go away, no matter how much you pray? Have you been supernaturally healed by God's power but later lost that healing, and now you want it back? Are you tired of being tired?

There is a *lot* of Bible teaching on healing out there, and there is a *lot* of research data floating around. Do you ever give up trying to sift through all that information to reach the level of abundant life (John 10:10) that Jesus teaches?

If you answered "yes" to any of these questions, this book is for you!

Here you will learn straightforward and efficient bio-hacks that incorporate cutting-edge science with the wisdom God gave us thousands of years ago in the Bible. You will learn how to get healed to reach—and remain—at the level of health you were created for.

This really is biblical. In Jesus' earthly ministry, He combined the natural with the supernatural to produce many of His healings and miracles. More on that in Chapter 2.

Benefit From the Best of Both Worlds

When I was so sick, I tried with some success many of the current data-supported biohacks as well as the ancient remedies that were backed by science. As I carefully combed through the Bible, looking for clues to healing and health, I discovered complementary underlying principles between healing in the Bible and current medical treatments.

When I combined them, I discovered I could get swifter results than either prayer or natural medicine alone.

It was so exciting to get all these healings; I couldn't help praying for others, many of whom also got healed. Later I began to teach this to others and my students began to see miracles, too.

Thus, this book series is being created to teach you the most data- and Bible-supported biohacks I've discovered. The process is very fluid and will become second nature with practice.

Your Step-by-Step Journey

To help you learn these biohacks and the principles they are based on, I've laid out the process in steps. By the end of the book, you will have biblically biohacked away many of your nagging health issues! Not only will you experience healing and regeneration miracles in your body, but—*with your healthcare practitioner's okay*—you will most likely be able to discontinue one or more prescription medications.

Moreover, you will experience the wonderful "side effects" of:

- Feeling decades younger
- Greater strength and flexibility in your body
- Experiencing deep peace for longer periods of time
- Brain fog lifting
- Greater creative flow
- Hearing God better

As I combined the natural with the supernatural, some conditions healed faster while others took longer. I researched the lives of great men and women of God who saw many miracles and healings and learned how important it is to deal with spiritual hindrances as the Holy Spirit reveals them to us.

Introduction

As director of a non-denominational church prayer ministry team, I've seen hundreds get healed and—to my sadness—many more *not* get healed. As I said earlier, we don't know why everyone doesn't get healed. My heart aches for the unhealed, which is why I scour the Bible for answers.

The Bible does give us *some* reasons why people aren't healed. I've seen that once the main hindrances were out of the way, rapid and lasting healing occurred.

In Chapters 6 and 7, you will learn very joyful ways to overcome most of the known hurdles. Later in this book, I will show you how engaging in high praise according to the keys in Psalm 149 will greatly increase your intimacy with the Lord, which can remove even more hindrances to healing. I've had several spontaneous healings that I never even asked for while in that special, personal place with Him.

From Science to Ministry

As a young adult, I started a career path in science because I wanted to heal people. Eventually, I moved into ministry and discovered that healing came so much faster. I thought that switching gears in mid-life set me back, especially since science and ministry seemed so disparate.

Now I realize that my science background (biology, chemistry, and microbiology), the ministry and Bible credentials I later earned (licensed, ordained pastor, and a certificate in the Hebrew context of the Bible), three decades of teaching both science and Bible subjects to students from five to seventy-five, and my desperation to get healed placed me in the unique position to develop and teach the best of both worlds. God worked out all those challenges for good!

A New Way Forward

There's actually no such thing as the "homeostasis" you learned in high school biology. Everyone is always moving in one direction or the other: toward an active, productive, healthy life or toward disability and even premature death. Nothing stays the same.

The U.S. is going backward in health, not forward. Death rates from adult diseases are steadily rising. The U.S. ranks *twenty-eighth* in health status among forty-two developed nations.[i] Six in ten adults in the U.S. have a chronic disease that is one of the leading causes of death and disability.[ii]

What about Christians? Religiously active people in the U.S. do not seem to be any healthier than the rest of the population, according to a Pew poll that measured obesity and frequency of exercise.[iii]

Introduction

Why this decline in health? Experts cite toxins, un-healthy diet, and stress. Our bodies must deal with thousands of times more toxins in our food and environment than our ancestors did even a hundred years ago. Our eating habits are very different from what our bodies were designed to handle. Plus, modern life doesn't encourage us to decompress from all the com-mitments, distractions, deadlines, and choices we are faced with multiple times a day.

"Moderation in all things" no longer works like it did for our grandparents. The toxic soup bowl we live, eat and breathe in, and the toxic thoughts in the media, the peo-ple around us, and in our own brains break us down faster than we can repair.

Clearly, what we're doing is not working very well. We need to change our strategy—fast. None of us has dec-ades to wait for spiritual or research breakthroughs. And for Christians, we have The-Break-through-of-the-Universe living in us! It's time for a new way forward.

Unless we learn how to counteract the eroding effects of modern life faster than they affect us, our bodies move backward through the health spectrum, even re-sulting in premature death. Why should we accept spending the last decade or two of our lives infirmed and disabled when there is a better, faster, cheaper and biblical way?

Jesus gave a good example of being on guard to actively defend spiritual health. I believe this can apply to our physical health as well, especially when we use spiritual means to gain healing:

> *"'I am the vine, you are the branches. He who abides in Me, and I in him, bears much fruit; for without Me you can do nothing'"* (Jn. 15:5).
>
> *Catch...the little foxes that spoil the vine"* (SOS 2:15).

The little foxes nibble away at our spiritual and physical health. This book gives you the biblical and data-driven tools to catch and stop those little thieves.

My heart aches when I watch Christians slowly slide toward disability, and they just accept it as part of life. That is so unnecessary! There is a much better way.

I learned this alone, thinking I would die before my kids graduated. But you don't have to slide that close to death or even be as tired and in constant pain like I was. You can quickly learn what took me years to figure out.

You're Invited!

I invite you to join me on this fun, joy-filled, and life-giving journey. You probably already have a lot of Bible and even scientific knowledge in your head. But knowledge is not power—it is only *potential* power. By picking up this book of life-changing technology, you are already halfway there. Congratulations!

Come like a child. Children have fun and are open to learning, so they learn quickly. While you are reading this new approach to healing, temporarily forget what you already know. Let the Holy Spirit sweep away old paradigms and the man-made doctrines and traditions you've accumulated so that you can discover our Father's goodness and infuse His vibrant life and age-less possibilities into your being.

Mark 4:24 says, *"Whatever you give ear to, will be given unto you."* In other words, the more carefully you listen and put into action what you hear, the more you will receive. There's a new way to robust health that's actually been there all along—it's just been underutilized in the body of Christ for far too long.

It is our privilege as believers to work in union with the all-powerful Creator of the universe. These biblical bio-hacks will radically change your life as they did mine. All it takes is a teachable heart. Let's get started!

Chapter 1

The Technology of Psalm 149

P salm 149 is only nine verses long and looks very simple. But it is packed with biohacks that are *uniquely* available to Christians.

There are many deep, scholarly commentaries on this Psalm, but what I'm teaching in this book is what I have put into practice so far.

Here is the whole psalm with twelve key phrases in bold to bring your attention to the biblical technology developed in this volume. (There's *more* in this little psalm that I am saving for another book.)

> *¹Praise the LORD!*
> *Sing to the LORD a **new** song,*
> *And His praise in the assembly of saints.*
> *²Let Israel **rejoice** in their Maker;*
> *Let the children of Zion **be joyful** in their King.*
> *³Let them praise His name with the **dance**;*
> *Let them **sing** [**make music**] praises to Him*
> *with the timbrel and harp.*
> *⁴For **the LORD takes pleasure in His people**;*
> *He will beautify the **humble** with salvation.*

*⁵Let the saints be **joyful** [**exult**] in glory;*
*Let them sing aloud on their **beds**.*
*⁶Let the **high praises** of God be in their **mouth** [**throats**],*
*And a **two-edged sword** in their hand,*
⁷To execute vengeance on the nations,
And punishments on the peoples;
⁸To bind their kings with chains,
And their nobles with fetters of iron;
⁹To execute on them the written judgment—
This honor have all His saints [faithful ones].
Praise the LORD!

Looking at the big picture, Psalm 149 begins and ends with the instruction to *"Praise the LORD."* This is often seen in Hebrew poetry and functions like two slices of bread to hold all the fixings of a tasty hamburger. (My apologies to vegetarians—this is a very good analogy otherwise. Think of the meat as being a really good pecan patty—my favorite meatless option.)

Verses one through five contain the condiments that go on top of the meat in the middle, verse six. The condiments in this psalm give the reader the needed keys to effectively engage in the meat of high praise plus the sword in order to bring a miracle into this physical world. The keys to engaging this extra power are:

- a new song

- joy
- gladness
- sound
- active movement
- the Lord's pleasure in us
- humility
- rest in Him

Verse six is the meat of this psalm, the sustenance, the focal point. It is high praise with a two-edged sword. You may be asking what is the difference between regular praise and high praise. I'm glad you asked. This is so important to understand that we'll take a deep dive into high praise in Chapter 3.

It is very interesting that the forms of all the Hebrew verbs in the first six verses are active, while all the verbs in the last three verses (except for the bottom *"Praise the Lord"* bun) are passive. These passive verses show the *results* of effectively engaging in the focus verse, high praise with the sword, using the keys given earlier.

So let's finish building our hamburger. We've opened the bun and piled the supplied condiments—the keys in this psalm—onto the top bread. When the meat patty is grilled to perfection and is sizzling and juicy, we pull it off the grill, set it onto the bottom bun, and close the burger.

The bottom bread soaks up the savory juices that passively seep out of the beautifully seasoned and grilled meat. In the same way, the last three verses in Psalm 149 reveal what happens—passively for us—in the spiritual realm to bring about the shifts, the biohacks, and the victory that were initiated by accurately engaging in high praise.

The human reader who chooses to actively engage in the focal point of this psalm, the high praises of God with the double-edged sword, does absolutely nothing more to bring about the victory. It's not our job to apply the vengeance, punishment, and binding described in verses seven through nine. We just get to enjoy the results of a supernaturally ordained burger: victory in our life!

Who, then, is carrying out those last three verses, defeating the enemy that is harassing us? Scripture elsewhere reveals that it is the angels who are doing the work of verses seven through nine (all emphases are mine):

> "Bless the LORD, you His angels, who excel in strength, who **do His word, Heeding the voice of His word.** Bless the LORD, all you His hosts, you **ministers of His,** who **do His pleasure**" (Ps. 103:20-21, emphases added).

"Are they not all ministering spirits sent forth to **minister for those** *who will inherit salvation?"* (Heb. 1:14, emphasis added)

"I am a **fellow servant with you** *and your brothers and sisters who hold firmly to the testimony of Jesus"* (Rev. 19:10 CSB, emphasis added).

The angels are fellow servants and we each have a part. Since we are the ones with the body and the indwelling Christ, our job is to engage in the high praise technology of verses one through six. Their job is to handle the human-activated spiritual swords, shackles, and chains to carry out the written judgments on spiritual wickedness in high places (Eph. 6:12).

Since there are so many instructions in scripture that cross-reference Psalm 149 (Psalms 146-150, 89:15, 103, 66:7 to name a few), these biohacks are arranged in a logical step-wise order.

As you follow the steps in this book, you will learn the biblical technology that all my biohacking volumes are based on and available only to believers: high praise, a new level of rest in Him, merging your heart and brain with God's intent, and activating the two-edged sword to its most effective level. You will also remove a major hindrance to healing.

You then learn some of the best data-supported bio-hacks that trigger parasympathetic nervous system dominance where biochemical changes and healing can take place. These biohacks are:

- specific breathing techniques
- Christian meditation
- sound and frequency
- heart-brain coherence

Each biohacking tool has an activation exercise and the opportunity to personalize it for your circumstances.
To help you master these tools and systematically pray for your needs, I suggest keeping a notebook to person-alize, plan, and track each biohack technique. I have produced a free *Companion Workbook* to download and print. You can get it at: TheHighPraise.com. If you put the pages in a 3-ring binder, you can always add more pages for additional prayer needs. As your healing miracles multiply, your written testimony of what God did for you will grow.

Keeping some kind of record will:

- Prevent you from being overwhelmed by all the needs around you, and keep you in rest, especially if you have several parts of your body that are in pain.

- Enable you to establish solid prayer habits, which lead to transformation.

- Encourage you, because you will be building solid evidence of what God has done for you, with you, and through you.

- Create for you a written testimony in *one place*, which will energize your faith (Philemon 1:6) and increase your intimacy with the Lord, which brings true transformation, not just improvement. When I started high praise, and the miracles began to happen regularly, I made the mistake of jotting them down anywhere—in my current journal, in the front of my Bible, or on scraps of paper. After a few years, these testimonies were so scattered, I had to do a *major* paper sorting-journal combing project to gather them all into one file!

- Help you get really good at biblical biohacking because you will begin to connect how you prayed for different types of needs with the results you got.

- Empower you to put these new skills of faith-based biohacking to work in other areas of your life, based on *your own* personal evidence.

I strongly recommend focusing on one need at a time, even though they may all be related. I've found that when I pray for multiple healings at once, my prayers seem to get "diluted," and it takes longer to get any one thing healed. We see in Genesis 1 that God focused on one thing at a time when He created the world. When I imitated Him, I found that answers come much faster when I was razor-sharp focused on one need at a time.

It doesn't take much in the way of resources to biohack. This book, your Bible, a notebook (strongly recommended). To make it even easier, you can download and print the free *Companion Workbook* from my website that contains all the activations, prayers, praise, personalized scriptures, etc., with room for you to write notes, healing testimonies, or journal your progress. Go to: TheHighPraise.com.

If you've tried other prayer techniques or programs and just haven't been able to change your habits, then start with a serious commitment at the end of this chapter and open your calendar. This book will show you the rest.

Commitment to being teachable + habit + the power of God = transformation, not just improvement

Write in a twenty-minute appointment to pray this system for five weeks. (If time is in short supply, see the next tip below.) Establishing a new habit of spending just twenty minutes a day biohacking will bear a huge harvest of the robust health you want.

If you believe you just don't have the time, think over how you go through your day where you could find twenty extra minutes. Then ask the Holy Spirit what you can curtail to make room to establish a new habit and new skills. (I limited my email time and did not allow my-self to follow interesting rabbit trails until later in the day.)

You can invest your time now or spend the rest of your day, month, and even years fighting battles that you otherwise wouldn't be facing. This small time investment has the biggest payout!

Find that time slot and write it into your calendar like physical therapy appointments. If you broke your leg and your doctor prescribed daily therapy, you'd make time, wouldn't you? How much more important is it to get infused with God and His nature every day so your whole body can get healed and refreshed?

If you need in-person guidance, check my website (TheHighPraise.com) or facebook.com/groups/chris-tianbiohacking for when the next online live mentoring group begins. Each module lasts five weeks, and there is a Q&A at the end of every session.

As Psalm 149:9 says, "this is the glory [some transla-tions say honor] of *all* the saints." That's *you*, the everyday believer of every denomination and every life-style. God has chosen to spread His heavenly kingdom to the earth through *you*.

If you haven't already, commit to a season of renewing your mind, of being teachable, to transform your health. This is the day! To make it authentic, sign and date the short commitment prayer in the activation below. An-gels are witnessing this, and the Holy Spirit will help you follow through.

You can do this! Psalm 149 gives us all the keys we need to give the angels what they need to slice and dice the enemy that's harassing you and stealing your health. You already have this book.

ACTIVATION: Prayer to Commit

"Father, Son, and Holy Spirit, before You and all Your heavenly hosts, I commit to a season of being teachable, to renewing my mind with your Word, to learning what high praises truly are and how to engage in them. Please give me a willing heart. Open the eyes of my heart so I can see you more clearly and know You more deeply. I desire for Your kingdom to come and Your will to be done here on this part of the earth where You placed me, as it is already done in heaven. Amen."

Signed,

_____ on this __ day of _____, 202_

Now mark down daily twenty-minute appointments in your calendar for the next five weeks and get started! Biohacking your body and mind—getting healed with science and the Bible—is a *lot* of fun. It is also a glory and an honor that God wants to bestow on you.

Chapter 2

Jesus' Ministry is Perfect Doctrine

Our great model, Jesus, combined the natural with the supernatural to produce many of His healings and miracles in His earthly ministry. Here are some examples:

- In John, Chapter 2, Jesus started with six 20–30 gallon jugs of water used for Jewish purification and turned the water into wine.

- All three synoptic gospels record Jesus starting with a few fish and loaves, then multiplying them to feed thousands.

- Jesus used His saliva several times:

  o Near Decapolis, He put His saliva in the deaf man's ears and then on his tongue (Mk. 7:33).
  o He spit on the eyes of the blind man of Bethsaida then put His hands on him (Mk. 8:23).
  o Near Siloam, Jesus *"spat on the ground and made clay with the saliva; and He anointed the eyes of the blind man with the clay"* (John 9:6).

Clearly, the divine Son of God didn't *need* physical starting materials to perform His miracles. Indeed, He performed many miracles with no starting materials. So why use physical matter at all?

We'll let the theologians debate it, but I have a hunch that He was simply modeling for us the many ways to do miracles. He was Emmanuel, God in man, and thus he used both the things man was formed out of as well as the supernatural, the God part, to produce miracles and healings.

There are many other examples in scripture of combining the two. The Israelite's second miracle in the Promised Land was a combination of natural and supernatural (or possibly supernatural timing) as well.

"When Joshua was by Jericho, he lifted up his eyes and looked, and behold, a man stood before him with his drawn sword in his hand; and Joshua went to him and said to him, 'Are you for us, or for our adversaries?' 'Neither,' he replied. 'I have now come as commander of the LORD's army.' Then Joshua bowed with his face to the ground in homage and asked him, 'What does my lord want to say to his servant?'" (Josh. 5:13-14)

At first, Joshua expected God to come to his rescue in a tough situation. But after the commander of the Lord's army spoke, Joshua realized that the angel didn't come to rescue him. The angel came to bring Joshua into alignment with God's ways.

When Joshua followed suit, he experienced his great-est, most miraculous victory. Through a combination of the natural (sound, vibration, frequencies[1] through si-lence, marching, shouting, and the trumpet) and the supernatural (the commander of the Lord's army, pos-sibly supernatural timing of an earthquake), the walls of Jericho collapsed.

Here are more biblical accounts of combining the natu-ral with the supernatural to produce a miracle or healing:

- Jacob peeled rods of green poplar, almond, and chestnut trees to cause his father-in-law's flocks to reproduce different types of coats and multiply the stronger animals (Gen. 30:37-43).

- Moses used a chunk of wood to make the bitter wa-ters at Marah sweet (Ex. 15).

- A raven fed Elijah meat and bread (1Ki. 17).

- Elisha threw flour in the pot to neutralize poison (2Ki. 4).

---

[1] If you're nervous about vibration and frequencies, you can jump to Chapter 9 for a sneak peek on the science and Bible behind it.

- Naaman dipped seven times in the Jordan river to be healed from leprosy (2Ki. 5).

Jesus Modeled high praise, as well. When the disciples asked Jesus to teach them how to pray, He started out with high praise of the Father: *"Our Father in heaven, Your name is holy"* (Mat. 6:9 NLV).

Jesus and His disciples were observant Jews. Every weekday, three times a day, they would have prayed a set of prayers that at that time were about four hundred years old, the Amidah. The Amidah is the central prayer of the Jewish liturgy. The first phrase of the Amidah, "Our Father in heaven," is what the opening prayer of the Amidah is all about, praising the God of the patriarchs, and then it praises Him for His power and might, raising the dead and healing the sick.

The phrase, "Your name is holy," is the next prayer in the Amidah to be recited and praises God's holiness and name.[iv]

As we will soon learn well in this book, the opening paragraphs of the Amidah are high praise! And this seems to be what Jesus was either referring to or drawing from when He taught his disciples to pray. 'Start every prayer with high praise,' He seems to be telling the disciples. That's a great mindset and lifestyle and one I strive to maintain.

"Since the word Jew (Yehudi) basically means, 'he who thanks God,' the entire life of a Jew consists of an on-going practice of blessing, praising, magnifying, and thanking God for His deeds," says Israel Bible Center professor Dr. Eli Lizorkin-Eyzenberg.[v] As an observant Jew, thanking, blessing, praising, and magnifying God's name would have been a lifestyle for Jesus and would have been flowing out of Him much of His time on earth.

We can also see in the gospels that Jesus *developed* authority. Luke 2:52 tells us that *"Jesus increased in wisdom and stature, and in favor with God and men."* The Greek word for "stature" not only means physical height but can also be a "metaphor of an attained state fit for a thing."[2] Then we don't hear anything more until He is ready to begin his ministry at about age thirty.

If you read about Jesus' miracles in the general chronology that scholars worked out, we can see a pattern of how Jesus' authority increased:

- **Over natural elements:** First changing water to wine, then quieting raging seas, and later walking on water.
- **In creative miracles:** He multiplied increasing amounts of food, and when He needed temple tax

---

[2] *The Outline of Biblical Usage* by Larry Pierce

money for Himself and Peter, He knew where the fish was that had the coins in its mouth and perhaps influenced that fish to be caught by Peter.

- **In Healing:** First the fever in Peter's mother-in-law, then the blind man, then the lepers, and later a man born blind (which the Jews considered impossible for anyone but God to do).

- **Resurrection miracles:** First Jesus raised Jairus' daughter who was dead a few minutes, then the Nain boy who had been dead a few hours, to Lazarus who had been dead four days and stinketh, and finally, overcoming His own death through His eternal resurrection for Himself and all those who receive Him.

Just as each of Jesus' healings and miracles were a step to the next level of miracles for Him, you and I can also develop our spiritual understanding and authority over nature, disease, and death.

Like infants who learn to walk, we have to grow, exercise, and train in order to one day run with a varsity track team. Jesus did this, and Psalm 149 shows us important training elements that increase our understanding and authority.
While I'm not "there" yet, I can tell you from experience that this is a very pleasant process. There is so much to

learn and enjoy! Let's pray a quick prayer to set our heart's desire to understand and follow Jesus' example.

ACTIVATION: Prayer to Follow Jesus' Model

"Father, Son, and Holy Spirit, thank You for guarding and protecting the holy scriptures over the centuries so that I can learn how Jesus and other men and women of God grew in wisdom, stature, and favor with You and mankind.

"Open the eyes of my heart to develop my spiritual understanding and authority over natural elements, over sickness, injury and disease, over creative miracles, and even over death. Lead me to fellowship with, learn from, and spur on those of like precious faith.

"Thank You—You are so loving and kind to provide everything I need to grow in Kingdom understanding and authority, just like Jesus did. Amen."

Now let's continue our journey and find out why Jesus taught us to begin with high praise.

Chapter 3

High Praise is Rocket Fuel

The first and most important step you must take is to understand that high praise is a specific technology that God has given us to defeat the devil that is messing with us. In this book, we engage in high praise to heal the infirmities and energy drains we get from living in a fallen world.

Regular praise has its time and place. But when we either don't know how to intentionally engage in high praise, are unaware of the power in high praise, or it doesn't readily flow from our hearts, regular praise becomes the default. If high praise is implemented at all, it's usually by a happy accident.

High praise is the high power that God makes available to us. Indeed, as we briefly saw in Chapter 1 and will revisit later, it is our *honor* to use this technology (Ps. 149:9). The purpose of this book is to teach you how to engage in high praise to heal your body, so let's set regular praise aside and continue.

We can use high praise alone to get healed, or we can use it in partnership with the world's science-backed biohacking techniques. High praise works like rocket fuel by lifting our minds off the earth into the heavenly places where we are seated with Christ (Eph. 2:6), so we can draw God's eternal, spiritual power back into our earthly circumstances that are within time.

What exactly is high praise? How does it differ from regular praise? Study the table on the next page, which was garnered from a study of power praise in scripture:

High Praise	High Praise Example	Regular Praise Example
Magnifies God's characteristics and nature.	"You are glorious, You are mighty, abounding in mercy and loving kindness."	"I praise You for your glory and might. I am amazed by Your mercy and loving kindness."
Addresses God directly.	"You are loving and kind."	"He is loving and kind."
Only speaks of the heavenly, eternal realm.	"You are the King of kings," "You are the author of salvation."	"Though the enemy closes in around me, You are my salvation and victory."
Excludes the speaker's earthly circumstances.	"You are the true source of light for all."	"Through all this darkness, You are my light."
Excludes the speaker's emotions, resolve, will, reactions, etc.	"Your love and greatness conquer all." "Your great name will be proclaimed forever."	"I am engulfed by Your great love for me." "I will proclaim Your great name forever."

Notes:

- The use of language is important. When we address God in the third person (*"He is great"*) rather than directly (*"You are great"*), we pull our attention off God to talk *about* Him to each other.

- When we use the words "me," "myself," or "I," or speak about our temporary earthly emotions or circumstances, we draw attention away from God to look at ourselves or our situation instead of Him. This waters down our praise. We bring the full power of God into our body and our circumstances by magnifying whatever aspect of God's nature we need, *not* by bringing attention to our temporary situation.

One of the best examples in the Bible of people successfully using high praise to powerfully and soundly defeat the enemy is in 2Chronicles 20:1-30 when a great multitude came against King Jehoshaphat. If you read the whole passage, you'll find that it echoes many of the components of Psalm 149.

There's a lot to learn in this passage, but let me give you the essentials for high praise:

Jehoshaphat with all of Judah (*which means "praised"*[3])

———————————————

[3] Gesenius' Hebrew-Chaldee Lexicon

stood before the Lord, asked Him to judge the enemies coming against them, then waited. God told them through the prophet Jehaziel (*"who looks to God"*[3]), son of Zechariah *("whom Jehovah remembers"*[3]), son of Benaiah (*"whom Jehovah has built"*[3]) to not to be afraid of the great multitude, but to just stand still because the Lord will fight this battle. At that word, they bowed and worshiped with loud and high voices (verses 18 and 19).

The next morning, the king humbled himself and consulted "the people." No high-ranking person is mentioned here. The king didn't ask the worship leaders what they learned at the latest conference. As a result of checking with generic "people," Jehoshaphat appointed ordinary singers (again, no top Davidic protégés are mentioned) to go out in front of the army and sing **to** the Lord and praise His **holiness**:

"After taking counsel with the people, he stationed singers to the LORD **extolling the One majestic in holiness** *as they went forth ahead of the vanguard, saying, "Praise the LORD, for His steadfast love is eternal"* (JPS, emphasis added).

Ordinary people advised the king of Judah (the king of praise) to set the singers in front of the army and have them *"praise the splendor of his holiness"* (CSB), or *"praise the LORD for his holy power"* (CEV). They needed power, so they praised him for his power and put the praisers in front of the physical army to face the enemy *first*.

The effect? The enemies of Jehoshaphat turned on one another and utterly destroyed each other in a bloody battle. Not one survived. The army did absolutely nothing to defeat the enemy; they just carried away the jewelry and other valuables.

In short, when faced with an overwhelming threat, they used high praise instead of fighting in the natural. This caused the enemy to turn on themselves and destroy each other. That echoes Psalm 149, and it's a *powerful* lesson for all of us!

Here are just ten of the many Bible verses that describe the effects of praise in their perfect standard. These scriptures reveal much of what is occurring in the spiritual and physical realm. Some scriptures are paraphrased:

- **Praise builds a throne for God to sit on.** *"But You are holy, enthroned on the praises of Israel* (Ps. 22:3 CSB).

- **The King arrives with His entourage.** *"He rode on a cherub and flew; he came swiftly on the wings of the wind"* (Ps. 104:3-4 ESV). Kings normally do not travel alone—their entourage comes with them. God's angels carry His thick, heavy presence to the throne we created with our praise of Him.

- **We experience joy.** *"In Your presence is fullness of joy"* (Ps. 16:11). You can't be sad when every hair follicle on your skin is aware of His presence.

- **Fear is thrust out.** *"God is love"* and *"perfect love casts out fear"* (1 Jn. 4:8, 18). The Greek word translated "cast" is an intense, violent action. Fear is "thrust" out the door when Love comes onto the scene, whom you are now acutely aware of because you praised Him in the highest form.

- **Despair and depression are driven out.** *"A garment of praise for a spirit of heaviness"* (Is. 61:3). Truly praising Him is a God-given technology for driving out despair and depression.

- **You are strengthened.** *"With praises from children and from tiny infants, you have built a fortress"* (Ps. 8:2a CEV).

- **The enemy is muzzled.** *"It makes your enemies silent, and all who turn against you are left speechless"* (Ps. 8:2b CEV).[4]

---

[4] The Hebrew word translated "silent" means "to cause to fail, to repose, allow to be lacking, to put down, take away."

- **The enemy is confused and scattered.** *"Praise brings confusion into the enemy camp and scatters the individuals"* (2Chr. 20).

- **The enemy is ambushed and destroyed.** *"When they began to sing and praise* (in holy priestly garments, v. 21)*, the LORD set ambushes against their enemies..."* and *"utterly killed and destroyed them"* (2Chr. 20:22, 23). NOTE: *'First the natural, then the spiritual'* (1Cor. 15:46 paraphrased). What was true physically for the Israelites up to the death and resurrection of Christ is true spiritually for us after that epoch-changing point in time.

- **The praiser gains inner radiance, strength, and God-awareness.** *"Blessed are those who have learned to acclaim You, who walk in the light of Your presence, LORD. They rejoice in Your name all day long, they celebrate your righteousness. For You are their glory and strength"* (Ps. 89:15-17 NIV). One translation says, *"they look to Him with uplifted, radiant faces."* It looks like a free facelift to me!

- **We become radiant and are esteemed.** *"Those who look to him are radiant, and their faces shall never be ashamed"* (Ps. 34:5). Another free facelift for those who fulfill verses 1-3, praising *Him*, magnifying *Him*, exalting the name of Yahweh in *humility*.

The effects of regular praise are powerful—like gasoline in automobiles that enable us to zip across the surface of the earth at seventy miles an hour and more. Because of the combustion engine, we can do so much more and go so much farther than if we were on foot, horseback, or buggy.

If you believe that God's Word always works, but you're not seeing the effects that scripture says you get when you praise Him, then perhaps it's time to re-think your definition of praise. So let's look at some more scriptures:

"The high praises of God" (Psalm 149:6).

The tense and aspect of the word translated "high praises" means the continuous, imminent, overhanging, overarching exaltation and lifting up of God. Wow—praise on steroids! It is the strongest form of praise in the Bible. High praise is *so* powerful and important that the psalmist uses six verses to describe how to engage in it.

If *regular* praise is like gasoline to shoot us across the earth's surface, *high* praise is like rocket fuel to propel you through the heavens where your answer is, where God has *"raised us up together, and made us sit together in the heavenly places in Christ Jesus"* (Eph. 2:6). That's where your answer is, and you can't access it when you are tethered to the earth.

Colossians 3:2 says, *"Set your mind on **things above** and not on **things on the earth**."* Here we see a distinction between the spiritual and earthly realms. Paul doesn't even qualify it with "most of the time, set your mind."

So then, *"the high praises of God"* is one hundred percent focused on The Most High God, His nature, and His marvelous deeds and creations—everything "high," everything eternal.

High praise is high. It does not include low things. What is low? Things on the earth such as temporary emotions, current circumstances, or insertions from the human ego—me, myself, and I. All these are the result of the fall of Adam and will pass away. These things of the earth may be true for this moment in time, but they are not eternal Truth. We cannot access our answer through earthly things. Our answer—the Way, the Truth, and the Life—is in the spiritual realm.

Paul lived this. In addition to Colossians 3:2 above and other New Testament scriptures, we'll see later, he also taught, *"I have been crucified with Christ; it is no longer I [ego] who live, but Christ lives in me; and the life which I now live in the flesh I live by faith in the Son of God, who loved me and gave Himself for me"* (Gal. 2:20).

That's not to say we can never use "me, myself, or I" in prayer when making declarations, when thanking God, or when talking to God during your day. I do that all the time. But when we want to "open the heavens" so to speak and get some victory, Psalm 149 teaches us that high praise is our "go-to" to get the job done. *"This is the honor of all the saints"* (Ps. 149:9, emphasis added).

I'm not the first or only one outside the Bible who has learned the new song of high praise. This is an ancient understanding that has been overshadowed by our culture of "rights" and "individuality" in the last few hundred years. Many good things in society have come out of our assertion of self, but it is a hindrance to the power of a completely unified God flowing through us. "Self" breaks unity with God and with the body of Christ.

To use the body analogy, every liver, heart, or kidney cell needs to act in unity first with the other liver, heart, or kidney cells to function as a unified organ. Then each organ system needs to act in concert with the other organs in order to keep the whole body healthy.

Many of the writings of the desert fathers and canonized saints contain high praises of God. The Catholic church has collected volumes of books documenting the miracles, signs, and wonders they performed or that spontaneously occurred as a result of their lifestyle of high praise.

When the monks and priests sang what we call the Gregorian chants, many miracles and healings broke out. If you read the Latin-to-English translations of these chants, you will find much high praise.

When I was in my early twenties, I had suffered whiplash twice. For the next thirty years, I experienced frequent neck spasms in spite of physical therapy. One day I was particularly deep into high praise, which brought my heart into a place of intense awe of God. I lifted up my hands and whispered, "Oh Lord, You are *sooo* magnificent!"

With my arms still in the air, I felt my neck jerk sideways with a soft inner pop and a second jerk in the other direction with an inner pop. Suddenly my neck felt free and loose, and I moved it farther than I had in years.

I didn't think much more about it until months later when I had a concussion, and my doctor ordered an MRI of my head and neck. He read the report to me: "Your head is fine, but you have two ruptured discs in your neck that have healed." He leaned into me and said, "They don't do that!" God is so good! I've had no neck injury pain ever since that day when my heart was deep in worship and I uttered to Him just one brief phrase of high praise.

A similar thing happened a few years earlier. Decades

before, one of my ribs had been broken and pushed out a few inches along my abdomen. It healed that way and bothered me whenever I sat for too long. Physical therapy to loosen the scar tissue helped only a little, and I had been contemplating surgery to remove it. But when my mind was fully fixed on God and my heart was overflowing with joy in Him, that protruding portion of my rib instantly dissolved. Again, I didn't ask for it. But there is so much power in high praise that it just overflows and heals.

I could give you lots of testimonies, but let's keep moving. Now that you know what high praise is and what it does, the big question remains: How do we do it? So glad you asked! Since music is so powerful, I'd like to say, "turn on some praise music and sing along."

Unfortunately, it is exceedingly difficult to find pure high praise songs that guide your heart to focus solely on the attributes and nature of God where His power is. Even the old traditional hymns regularly pull your mind back to things on the earth. Out of more than two thousand contemporary and traditional songs labeled "worship" or "praise" that I have screened, less than 4% were entirely high praise. Ninety-six percent of these songs pulled the listener's attention away from God with lyrics that described temporary earthly circumstances, emotions, or various states of "me, myself, and I."

Here are ten songs that contain only high praise and the artist or group that popularized them:

- *Blessed are You,* Paul Wilbur
- *Countless Wonders,* Chris Tomlin
- *Jesus This is You,* Chris Tomlin
- *King of Glory*, Jesus Culture
- *Magnificent,* Hillsong or Michael Chenoweth
- *Most High God,* Paul Wilbur
- *Oh What Love,* Keith Duncan
- *Unto You,* Roy Fields
- *You Alone*, John G. Elliott
- *You Do All Things Well,* Chris Tomlin

My whole list is in the free *Companion Workbook* that you can download from: TheHighPraise.com.

But even without recorded music, you can still raise your praise to the highest level. It just takes a little preparation and intention until your soul gets infused with the high praises of God. At that point, they become second nature and flow back out of you.

Since high praise brings the King (Ps. 22:3), there is a protocol to observe. But high praise is also a lifestyle that richly deepens as your relationship with God and His nature becomes etched into your being. This activation exercise will get you started on the journey of a lifestyle of high praise. It is longer than the other activations because this is so fundamental to breaking free of the earth's pull.

ACTIVATION: Fill Up with Rocket Fuel

Before & After Inventory to Train Your Senses

Before and after the first dozen or so times you do these activations, take this quick inventory of what you are sensing in your body and mind. This will enable you to train yourself to detect His Kingly presence and His angelic entourage so you can distinguish them from everything else.

- Breathing: Slow? Even? Shallow? Easy? Difficult?
- Mind: Distracted? Focused? Racing? Bored? Alert?
- Skin exposed to the air: Cool? Hot & dry? Sweaty?
- Skin under your clothing: Cool? Hot & dry? Sweaty?
- Stomach: Calm & relaxed? Jittery?
- Muscles: Relaxed? Calm? Tense? Jittery?
- Heart: Quiet? Beating hard? Tension? Ease?
- Pain level: (none) 0-1-2-3-4-5-6-7-8-9-10 (worst)
  Location:_____
- Energy level: (none) 0-1-2-3-4-5-6-7-8-9-10 (highest)

---

1. **The Blood of Jesus.**

   Jesus is the only door, and it is only by the blood of Jesus that we can come into the Most Holy Place (Heb. 10:19). Slowly speak this or something similar out loud:

   "I cover myself and my whole family, _____
   (name them), *with the blood of Jesus. Thank you,*

Father, for the sprinkling of Jesus' blood that gives me boldness to come before Your throne of grace" (from Heb. 5:13).

2. Forgive.

It's a choice, not a feeling. You may even need to forgive yourself—there must be *no regrets* in your heart![vi]

"By an act of my will, I choose to forgive _____ *(name/s) for* _____ *(offense). I release them to You, Father, and ask that You bless them."*

3. Thanksgiving.

"Enter His gates with thanksgiving and into His courts with praise" (Ps. 100:4). We express gratitude for what someone has done for us. When thanking God, it is best to think of yourself as a group rather than an individual. This keeps your attention off of your individual self. The reality is that you are the body of Christ in union with all other believers.

Also, consider that thanksgiving usually affects the heart on a deeper level when you thank Him for spiritual things that money cannot buy, rather than physical things that can be purchased. Salvation is the greatest gift and can bring the deepest joy when we understand it well.

Read this slowly, out loud, savoring and thinking about each phrase:

"Thank you, Father, for canceling the charges that stood against us and condemned us. You completely removed them all, nailing them to the cross! And having disarmed the powers and authorities, You made a public spectacle of them, triumphing over them by the cross!" (from Col. 2:14)

4. High Praise.
Slowly, thoughtfully, speak out loud these high praises of God from scripture—what He says about Himself.

You don't need to breeze through all of these in one sitting. It is much better to focus on one bullet point each session. At this point, don't stray from the high praises below. (Later on, high praise will naturally flow out of you.) These high praises and many more are in the *Companion Workbook:* TheHighPraise.com

It helps to raise your hands or bow your head because this lines up your body with the truth and praise that you have chosen to express.

If you don't feel like praising Him at the moment, are not yet familiar with these characteristics of God, or even if you're a little disappointed, bewildered, or upset with

Him right now, you are still speaking the truth about Him when you speak these high praises. Just trust that the truth of God's loving Word will conquer every hesitation, ignorance, or fault.

As you slowly speak out these praises, at some point, your heart—the gateway between your soul and body—will line up with the truth of who God is. Sometimes it feels like you have to push through a heavy door. Other times it's very easy. But when you feel a "swelling of peace and love" or "fullness of joy" in your heart area, God has inhabited His praise, and you have entered into the state worship in spirit and in truth. This is what Jesus spoke about to the Samaritan woman at the well in John Chapter 4.

High Praise for…

- **God's Power.** *"Your right hand, LORD, has become glorious in power. Your right hand, LORD, has dashed the enemy in pieces. And in the greatness of Your excellency, You have overthrown those who rose up against You. Who is like You, LORD, among the gods? Who is like You, glorious in holiness, fearful in praises, doing wonders?"* (from Ex. 15)

- **God's Glory.** *"The heavens declare Your righteousness, and we see Your glory: Your honor, splendor, abundance, richness, and dignity. You, LORD, are high above all the earth. You are exalted far above* all gods. You preserve the lives of Your saints and deliver us out of the hand of the wicked. You sow Your light and gladness for Your people" (from Ps. 97:6,7,10,11).

- **His Rulership.** *"You are the living God and the immortal God, the everlasting King of ages. You are the invisible God, the true God, and the only God. Your throne, oh God, is forever and ever, and a scepter of righteousness is the righteous scepter of Your Kingdom. To You be all honor and glory forever and ever. Amen"* (from 1 Tim. 1:17; Ps. 45:6).

- **God's Holiness.** *"Holy, holy, holy, LORD God of hosts! Who was, and who is, and who is coming! You are the alpha and the Omega, the First and the Last, the Beginning and the End. There is no Rock like You"* (from Rev. 4:8; 21:6a; Sam. 2:2b).

- **His Creative Nature.** *"You, LORD, laid the foundation of the earth from the beginning, and the heavens are the works of Your hands. In Your hands, oh LORD, are the deep places of the earth. The strength of the hills is Yours, also. The sea is Yours, for You made it, and Your hands formed the dry land. You uphold the universe by the power of Your Word!"* (from Heb. 1:3b,10; Ps. 95:4,5).

- **God's Wisdom and Ways.** *Oh how deep are Your*

riches and wisdom and knowledge, oh King! Your judgments cannot be searched out, and Your ways are inscrutable—they are beyond finding out! All things are from You and through You, and to You. To You be the glory forever and ever Amen!" (from Rom. 11:33, 36).

- **God's Tremendous Love & Mercy.** *"You are Love, oh God! Thank You for showing Your love for us by sending Your only Son into the world to give us abundant life, by being the atoning sacrifice by which our sins are forgiven"* (from 1Jn. 4:8-10).

- **His Faithfulness.** *"Your steadfast love never ceases. Your mercies never come to an end—they are brand new every morning. How great is your faithfulness, oh God"* (from Lam. 3:22-23).

SELAH! Pause and think about it!

5. **Second Inventory.**
   Go back to the **Before and After Inventory to Train Your Senses** and check your bodily senses again. Note anything that changed.

6. **Prayer or Simple Biohack.**
   VERY IMPORTANT: Don't stop yet! By creating a throne for God to sit on (Ps. 22:3), you have just tapped into another realm and built up spiritual energy

in and around you. As a believer, He's in you and you're in Him (1Jn. 4:15) and He has *"raised us up together, and made us sit together in the heavenly places in Christ Jesus"* (Eph. 2:6). So exercise your authority over what you've been given. Choose one:

- **Pain.** If anything is still in pain, speak to that part of your body: "_____ (body part), *line up with the will of God and be healed. Receive His life, light, and love. Pain: go out. Life of God: flow in."*

  NOTE: Jesus did this—He spent time with the Father tapping into His will and receiving His spiritual energy. Then, as He went about the day, He spoke to the body parts or issues that people brought to His attention.

- **Health Issue.** If you have an ongoing health problem, speak to the body part. For example, if you have high blood pressure, say, "__*Arteries*__, *you are free of resistance and are normal and healthy. Healthy levels of nitric oxide are now being produced, and all my blood vessels are flexible and clear of plaque. Blood pressure, you remain in healthy normal ranges for all my activities of the day."*

NOTE: After just three weeks of spending a few minutes in high praise every day then speaking to my thyroid, I tapered entirely off thyroid meds and all tests are now normal. Please see your doctor before adjusting any of your prescription medications.

- **Declarations and decrees.** This is an excellent time to make your decrees, especially who you are in Christ. You're not doing this to convince your mind; you're making declarations about who you in Christ so that your body and the rest of creation begin to recognize the Creator in you. Thus, they will respond better to you. In the *Companion Workbook,* you will find a scriptural guide to identity decrees—who you are through the finished work of Jesus Christ: TheHighPraise.com

- **Use a biblical biohack.** Since this is a foundational training session, we'll just do a simple prayer of protection and prophecy from Psalm 91 regarding your new lifestyle of high praise and biblical biohacking:

  o *"Thank you, Father, Son, and Holy Spirit, for this precious time with you! Thank you for sending Your angels to watch over my family and me, to guard us, keep us in all our ways. Indeed, they shall bear us up in their palms lest we dash our feet against stones. We shall beat down and trample under our feet the lion and the snake."*

  o *"You say that because I have set my love upon You, that You will deliver me and set me on high because I intimately know Your name. I have called upon You and You have answered me. The great I AM is with me in every trouble, delivering and honoring me. Thank You for satisfying me with your salvation, deliverance, victory, welfare, health, comfort, security, safety, protection, and prosperity."*

If anything was healed from this activation, be sure to add it to: facebook.com/groups/christianbiohacking to bolster everyone's faith.

Daily homework to infuse high praise into your being so that it will flow back out:

1. Download from my website the free *Companion Workbook* that contains many high praises at: TheHighPraise.com. Write one or two praises a week on a sticky note or 3x5 card and keep it handy to read out loud during the day. Keeping one sticky note on your bathroom mirror, one on the window over the kitchen sink, and a 3x5 in your pocket. This will train your brain to keep your thoughts on things above (Col. 2:3). High praise will then become a lifestyle for you and it will freely flow from your heart, past your lips, and out into the atmosphere. That's when the healings really begin to flow. I call it "lifestreaming."

2. Spend the first five minutes of your twenty-minute biohack appointments in high praise. Establishing this habit of high praise before engaging in meditation, prayer, biohacking—anything—will be a major game-changer for everything you do.

3. Highlight in your Bible with a yellow-colored pencil high praises from the book of Psalms. (Do not highlight the first phrase in the psalms, i.e., *"A Psalm of Asaph."*) This will enable you to later flip through your Bible and quickly find some high praises for every devotional time or prayer meeting. A checklist of 36 pure high praise scripture references you can highlight is in the free *Companion Workbook at* TheHighPraise.com. This exercise will also teach you to spot high praise very easily.

We have filled up on rocket fuel, but we're not ready to launch yet—we need to incorporate another important habit into high praise, which is part of Psalm 149's instruction to speak the high praises of God from our *beds.* What does that mean?

Chapter 4

Breathing Life

The way we breathe triggers our bodies to either rest and repair, or fight or flee from danger. Learning to breathe in Jesus—the breath and author of life—accelerates healing and repair.

> *"And the LORD God…breathed into his nostrils the breath of life, and man became a living being"* (Gen. 2:7).

> *"It is He Himself Who gives life and breath and all things to all [people]"* Acts 17:25 AMPC).

> *"The Spirit of God has made me, and the breath of the Almighty gives me life"* (Job 33:4).

> *"Let everything that has breath praise the LORD"* (Ps. 150:6).

In *Breath: The New Science of a Lost Art,* [vii] author James Nestor does a great job of recapping the ancient and scientific approaches to breathing. In a nutshell, science has verified and measured what ancient masters have been practicing for centuries: when you change your breathing, you change your body's cellular and nerve chemistry.

Science has shown that lowering your breathing rate throughout most of your day and breathing through your nose instead of your mouth:

- Enables rest, relaxation, reproduction, and repair to occur in your body
- Lowers blood pressure
- Improves your carbon dioxide (CO_2) levels
- Lower heart rate
- Increases efficiency during exercise (a measurement of fitness)
- Increases heart rate variability (important for longevity)
- Increases energy
- Improves digestion
- Has a calming effect after five to ten minutes of doing this
- Restores lungs after a damaging incident if done five to ten minutes/day for about two months
- Enables learning and meditation states of mind by increasing blood flow to the brain and bringing brainwave activity into the alpha ("relaxed alert") range

The reason all these things occur when breathing is reduced is because slow breathing activates the parasympathetic nervous system – that's the mode needed for the rest, relaxation, reproduction, and repair functions of the body to turn on.

On the other hand, rapid breathing triggers the opposite, the sympathetic nervous system to dominate, which is your fight, flight, or freeze mode. This function can be harnessed for peak athletic performance and other purposes, but it's not healthy to remain in this state for long periods.

Unfortunately, our stress-filled lives trigger this mode to be dominant most of the time. This is why so many of the health gurus teach breath control in some form. Of course, they may also add in a bunch of New Age mumbo-jumbo, which we are wise to ignore. But let's not throw out the baby with the bathwater. They are right about the importance of breathing.

In Genesis 2:7, God created man using a different method from all the other animals. He breathed His breath of life into the man. The result is interesting: the better Hebrew translations say, *"man became a living soul."* Very cool! In 2Kings 4:18-37, the prophet Elisha raised the Shunammite woman's son from the dead by copying God in two ways: laying on him (a way of hovering and brooding as in Genesis 1:2) and breathing into his mouth.

When I was in my fifties, my blood pressure crept up a

little. I did some research and learned how to slow my breath to reduce blood pressure. Then, whenever I got rushed, stressed, or felt the telltale sign of rising blood pressure *(for me, it was little flitting head pains),* I did the slow breathing exercises while gently breathing/speaking out some scriptures on the breath of God.

Within three or four breathing cycles, my blood pressure dropped. Since the effect was only temporary and I wanted to teach my body to keep resetting into parasympathetic mode, I set the timer on my phone to go off every hour and labeled it, "How's my breathing?" If it was fast and shallow, I slowed it down with my new bio-hack. My blood pressure has been perfect ever since—and that was more than ten years ago.

Don't take my word for it; convince yourself. Find or borrow a blood pressure measuring device. (Many drugstores have a free booth where you can take your own readings.) Measure your blood pressure two times: first, when you've been breathing your usual rapid or shallow way, then after you've been breathing slowly (ten to twelve-second cycles—see the activation below) for a couple of minutes. You can also do this experiment in reverse to raise your blood pressure through rapid breathing.

The breathing gurus and even the average person can

get amazing results just by utilizing breathing techniques to trigger one branch of the nervous system or
the other. How much more can we believers achieve
when we consciously breathe in the breath of *Almighty
God*?

ACTIVATION: Breath of Life

Before & After Inventory to Train your Senses

This isn't part of the biohack, but while you're training your senses to more acutely detect the spiritual realm and its effect on your body, continue to take before and after inventories, making quick notes in your notebook:

- Breathing: Slow? Even? Shallow? Easy? Difficult?
- Mind: Distracted? Focused? Racing? Bored? Alert?
- Skin exposed to the air: Cool? Hot & dry? Sweaty?
- Skin under your clothing: Cool? Hot & dry? Sweaty?
- Stomach: Calm & relaxed? Jittery?
- Muscles: Relaxed? Calm? Tense? Jittery?
- Heart: Quiet? Beating hard? Tension? Ease?
- Pain level: (none) 0-1-2-3-4-5-6-7-8-9-10 (worst)
  Location: _____
- Energy level: (none) 0-1-2-3-4-5-6-7-8-9-10 (highest)

Note about breathing. The goal in this breathing exercise is *slow,* controlled breathing. You do not want to breathe particularly deep. Rapid breathing and breathing too deep, too fast can cause hyperventilation and dizziness. This occurs because carbon dioxide (CO_2) has been exhaled too fast, causing a drop in your blood CO_2 levels.

1. **Create and focus your intent.**
   Scan the list below, Benefits of Slow Breathing, and mark ONE thing per session that you want to improve. Some improvements occur almost immediately, but others take several weeks. (I've removed

from this list the benefits that we are not normally aware of or cannot measure at home.)

BENEFITS OF SLOW BREATHING:
- Improved rest, relaxation.
- Improved reproduction
- Lower blood pressure. Current measurement: _____ / _____
- Reduce heart rate. Current resting bpm: _____
- Increased efficiency during exercise (less wind-edness, improved fitness).
- Increased energy
- Improved digestion
- Improved learning (better or longer focus)
- Improved meditation state (i.e., deeper state, faster to enter meditative state)
- Calming effect over anxiety (Data indicates this takes 5-10 minutes)
- Restore lungs after a damaging incident _____(describe)_____. (The data indicates the reduced breathing exercise below can heal the lungs if done for 5-10 minutes per day for about two months. But the Breath of Life Himself can do it even faster.)

2. **Breathing biohack + the Breath of Life.**
Now infuse the Breath of Life into your being by combining a science-supported breathing biohack

with meditating on specific scriptures.

At first, you'll need a timer with a seconds indicator until you learn what a 12-second breathing cycle (5 breaths per minute) feels like. If applicable, put your hands on anything in the focus-intent list above that you marked for improvement, such as on your abdomen for digestion, your head for a better meditative state, etc.

Now shift your focus to Jesus and say out loud: *"Thank You, Jesus, for Your finished work on the cross"* and begin your breathing cycles:

- Slowly inhale through your nose over five seconds.
- Hold one second.
- Exhale over five seconds while saying the first personalized scripture:
  - *"Your breath makes me a living soul"* (from Gen. 2:7).
  - *"You give me life and breath in all things"* (from Acts 17:25).
  - *"Your breath of life permeates every cell in my flesh"* (from Gen. 6:17).
  - *"The breath of God invigorates me"* (from Rev. 11:11).
  - *"Your breath, Almighty God, gives me life"* (from Job 33:4).
- Pause one second.

You have now completed one, twelve-second round.

- Repeat the steps above, speaking out loud the next personalized scripture until you have gone through all five scriptures.

This makes one minute at the breathing rate of five breaths per minute.

- Repeat the five breath cycles above at least four more times, for a total of five minutes. If you need deeper healing like lung restoration, do this for ten minutes.

3. **Close.**
   "Thank you, God, for Your breath of Life. I praise You for Your gift of life."

Take Your Second Sensory Inventory. Quickly assess the state of your sensory functions in your body and jot them down in your notebook.

Go back to the item you marked in the *Benefits of Slow Breathing* **list** and note or measure (if applicable) any changes.

Do this exercise as often as you can every day until you catch yourself breathing well throughout the day. You might want to set a timer to remind yourself until this becomes a habit.

When I developed this biohack, there were no technologies to help. But now there are many YouTube guided breathing videos, and even Fitbit has a two- and five-minute guided breathing experience called "Relax." There are probably other apps as well.

If anything was healed from this activation, be sure to add it to the Christian Biohacking Facebook group so your faith will be energized even more, and others' faith will be bolstered: facebook.com/groups/christianbiohacking.

So far, we've learned the high praise foundation; then we stacked breathing the breath of life to facilitate the shift into *rest and repair mode* and resting in Him. In both of these, we briefly mentioned intent. Now it's time to learn how to create an "intention blueprint."

Using our rocket metaphor, you stepped into your rocket through the door, Jesus Christ, when you were born from above. Scripture is your rocket, the structure that takes you into spiritual space. High praise is your fuel to blast you off the earth to take you to your destination. But where exactly are you going? What does it look like? What flight path will you take?

Chapter 5

Biblical Meditation
Forms Divine Intent

Biblical meditation forms a spiritual blueprint on which your miracle or biohack will take physical shape. This kind of meditation takes your desire for God's power to work in your life and shapes it into intent. Let's see how the woman with the issue of blood formed intent from her desire to be healed.

> *"Sing to the LORD a **new** song"* (Ps. 149:1b, emphasis added).

> *"For **she kept saying**, 'If I only touch His garments, I shall be restored to health'"* (Mark 5:28, emphasis added).

> *"For she **kept saying to herself**, If I only touch His garment, I shall be restored to health"* (Mat. 9:21 AMPC, emphasis added).

The opening verse in Psalm 149 tells us to sing a *new* song. "New" in scripture is not just an improvement on the former: the old has been completely wiped out.

*"If anyone is in Christ, he is a **new creation; old things have passed away;** behold, **all things have become new**"* (2Cor. 5:17, emphases added; see also Gal. 6:15). *"For behold, I create **new** heavens and a **new** earth; **and the former shall not be remembered** or come to mind"* (Is. 65:17, emphases added).

Therefore, a *new* song is something that comes out of a new mindset and a transformed heart. The old heart is gone; the old ways are gone. Scripture is telling us to totally change the song we sing, to change our definition of praise.

Psalm 149:1 also instructs us to sing this new song *to the LORD.* This indicates that our mind's eyes should be completely on Him. We're not singing this song to our friends *about* Him.

To sing this new song, the desire to transform has to drop from our mind into our heart, where intent forms. Then out of the abundance of intent in the heart, we frame our intent with the language that comes out of our mouth. At that point, our body chemistry or circumstances begin to change.

In the case of the woman with the issue of blood for twelve years (Mat. 9:20-22, Mk. 5:25-34, and Lk. 8:43-46), most translations say, *"**she said,** 'If I only touch...'"* That sounds like she said it once, then pressed through the crowd and touched Jesus.

But a few English translations bring out the nuance of the Greek form of the verb that expresses continual or repeated action. This makes a big difference in understanding how the woman got her miracle. *"She kept saying..."* The woman kept repeating over and over, perhaps barely audibly in Mark's account. Matthew's account specifically says, *"she kept saying to herself."*

We have two witnesses here, and I don't believe they contradict. Instead, they reveal a dual process. First, the woman internally meditated on what she wanted. Then she formed her intent regarding how she was going to get her healing (*"when I touch His clothes, I shall be made well,'"* Mk. 9:28), and what it would feel like (she felt in her body that *"the fountain of her blood was dried up,"* verse 29). With her mouth, she released her intent, and with her body, she pushed through the crowd to make contact with Jesus' garment.

The Bible exhorts us *many* times to meditate and often continues by telling us what to meditate on. There are many different words in the Bible for meditation, showing us that there are many ways to meditate. This is important! Biblical meditation causes us to focus on His will, His ways, His Kingdom. As one of my Bible teachers said, "Power flows where the will of the Father goes."

When you meditate on God's Word and His will, what happens is that His desires shape your desires. For example, you might read in the Word, *"Beloved, I pray that you would...be in health"* (3 John 2). So you think, "Hmmm, it's God's desire that I be in health. I would like to get healed of this pain in my back. That's a godly desire—it's in line with His will."

But the pain in your back is still there. When God created the world, He *saw* that it was in a state of chaos (Gen. 1:2), but He didn't *say,* "Oh, what a mess We've got!" Instead, He "framed" the world that He desired with His thoughts and then words. *"The worlds were framed by the word of God, so that the things which are seen were not made of things which are visible"* (Heb. 11:3).

We can see exactly how God framed up the world He desired by scanning Genesis 1, starting with verse 3: *"Let there be light... darkness... Let...dry land appear... grass... herb... seed... fruit."* Do you see how God spoke what He desired, not the chaos that He saw?

Likewise, you take your God-inspired desire to have your back healed and frame it up by thinking (meditating) to form your intent (what that looks like) and then speaking it out. You could say something like, "Let there be full range of motion in every direction my vertebra were created to move. Let there be pain-free movement in every way. All inflammation is gone and there is perfect circulation in my back. I have the bone density of a 20-year-old." Then your desire can manifest in the physical realm as healing in your back. Like a contractor building a house, a blueprint is necessary to build the house that *you* want.

The early Church fathers knew the value of meditation. Meditation forms the necessary "intent" that psychologists talk about.

Intriguing experiments in quantum physics have shown that matter can exist as a particle or a wave depending on what the observer intends or expects to see. *"Now faith is the substance of things hoped for, the evidence of things not seen"* (Heb. 11:1). Quantum physics approaches the faith realm, and intent is part of faith.[viii]

Dr. Joe Dispenza is an author, speaker and teacher who specializes in neuroscience. His research has taken him—among many areas—to study the science of meditation. His research has shown that "when you marry a clear intention (which is a thoughtful process) with an elevated emotion (a heart-felt process), you move into a new state of being and your body chemistry changes."[ix] He says that when you do this, you are unmemorizing old, negative thought patterns that have been harming your body, and you are memorizing new thought patterns that improve your body chemistry.

Even though He excludes God in his equations, I see Hebrews 4:12 all through his explanation:

> *"For the word of God is living and powerful, and sharper than any two-edged sword, piercing even to the division of soul and spirit, and of joints and marrow, and is a discerner of the thoughts and intents of the heart."*

Dr. Dispenza seems to have borrowed from Col. 3:2:

> *"Keep your mind set on things above* [where all the elevated emotions are] *not on things of the earth."*

…and from Phil. 4:8:

> *"Whatever things are true… noble… just… pure… lovely… of good report… virtuous and praiseworthy—meditate on these things"* (Phil. 4:8).

Dr. Dispenza may or may not know this, but he is repeating the biblical advice to keep your emotions in the elevated range. In scripture, I found *"Rejoice in the LORD" forty-eight* times! Joy—and the elevated emotions that often come with it—are *really* important to our well-being!

If the secular world can change their body chemistry by framing intent that is not based on God's will or Word, how much more can we Christ-carriers transform our body chemistry by framing our intent with God? We have the higher Word!

A new song to the Lord—a new frame of mind formed from intent for change—started for me with reading the Word and meditating on it. *"Be transformed by the renewing of your mind"* (Rom. 12:2). A new song begins with a transformed mind. And when our mind is transformed, it affects our body because the mind is designed to control the body.

Early in my desperate morning time with God, I wrote verses or phrases that seemed important onto note cards. During the day, I pulled them out of my pocket to mull them over in my heart, ask God questions, and look up similar verses. The next morning, I would personalize the verse as a prayer, confession, or praise. The revelation of high praise came out of those meditations.

This is one form of meditation that you've probably been doing for years.

Through each of these experiences, I understood God's nature and immense love on a deeper level. Creativity began to flow, and I started hearing melodies that perfectly fit the scriptures of God's nature that I was meditating on. I learned how to play piano just so that I could try to reproduce what I was hearing.

Can you see how the foundations of scripture (the rocket), meditation (flight deck programming), and high praise (rocket fuel) stack on each other?

In the activation below, you will learn just one out of the many Biblical ways to meditate.

ACTIVATION: Biblical Meditation to Form Intent

When you're up and running, you will meditate on scriptures that the Holy Spirit highlights for you or a Bible verse that you personalize for the current circumstance you are in. Since this is a training meditation and most of us could improve our posture at least a bit, we will meditate on that as a teaching tool.

1. **Prepare:**
    Write in your notebook or journal:

    *   My desire: *To improve my posture.*

    *   Scriptures:
        o   *"I will strengthen you, yes I will help you, I will uphold you with my righteous right hand"* (Isaiah 41:10).
        o   *"That our daughters may be as pillars sculptured in palace style"* (Ps. 144:12b).

2. **Begin by breathing to get into a meditative state of mind.**
    About five breaths per minute trigger the parasympathetic nervous system and shift your brain to produce predominantly alpha waves—a relaxed alert state.

    *   Inhale five seconds and hold one second.

- Exhale five seconds saying: *"You are the great, the mighty, and the awesome God"* (from Neh. 9:32) and hold one second.

- Inhale five seconds and hold one second.

- Exhale five seconds saying: *"Your faithful love endures forever"* (from Ps. 136:1).

- Repeat this for several cycles until you feel the shift into parasympathetic mode (your muscles relax a bit, you feel calmer, your mind slows down a bit, slower heart rate, etc.).

3. **Frame up your intent.**
   What does good posture look like? What parts of your body will change? Write it out to guide how you will speak it out:

   - *"My back is like a pillar fashioned for a palace, exquisitely formed."*

   - *"Each vertebra is strong and dense, and the Lord upholds each one."*

   - *"My muscles are strong with an abundant supply of mitochondria for energy."*

- *"The Lord invigorates the mitochondria in my muscle cells."*
- *"Stem cells are drawn to my back, multiply, and differentiate into bone, sinew, and muscle cells."*

- *"I move with ease and flexibility."*

4. Elevated emotion.

Now bring in a feeling of joy or love. What would it feel like to have a super strong and flexible back like a gymnast or a ballet dancer? How would it feel to move effortlessly? Hold onto the thought that brought the emotion. (If you can't imagine it, just bring in an elevated emotion with a thought that is not related to a strong back. It's the emotion you want.)

Try to sustain the emotion while focusing on your framed intent—marry the two. Now with that feeling of joy or love, go back to #3 above and slowly speak out what good posture looks like. If you lose the elevated emotion, just do an instant replay of what brought the elevated emotion in the first place. Your body chemistry already started to change a few seconds after you began this exercise, but you want to stay in this intent + elevated emotion for about seven or eight minutes to allow more and more metabolic pathways and systems to shift.

5. Close with thanksgiving.

"Thank you, God, for multiplying the mitochondria in the muscles of my back. Thank You for girding up each vertebra in my spine. Thank you for invigorating my whole body with Your strength and for making my back strong like a pillar, yet flexible like a vine."

Good job! It's difficult to marry intent with elevated emotion and keep it sustained for eight minutes. Even if you did it for thirty seconds, that's very good! You made some changes in your body today, and as you practice this skill, it will become much easier.

If anything was healed in this activation, be sure to add it to the Biblical Biohack Facebook group: facebook.com/groups/christianbiohacking to energize your faith and build up others' faith, too.

Let's develop our metaphor of the rocket.

You were created to divinely rule the earth and your circumstances from heavenly places. You heard it, you believed it, and you made the decision to get to a heavenly place in Christ (your desire). So you picked up your destination map (this book on biblical biohacking). You stepped through the door (Jesus) of your rocket ship (the Word of God) and are stocking it with the needed food, travel clothes, and equipment (specific scriptures that apply to your circumstance). Still doing your pre-launch tasks, you carefully check the galaxy map and program your route (meditation to frame-up intent). The fuel gauge indicates you have a full tank of rocket fuel (high praise).

There are still two other details to check off your list in order to have a successful trip: ground control and the launch pad.

Notice I didn't call it "mission control." As a believer, you and your mission are not of this world. When physical rockets are set up at the launch pad, they are stabilized and held upright by being bolted to what are called "hold-down arms."

So, ground control (the devil who was thrown to the earth) has bolted the hold-down arms (spiritual hindrances, negative emotions, emotional attachments, etc.) to your rocket, and they are working hard in an attempt to reprogram your flight plans, so you complete *their* missions for them (spreading sin, evil, etc.).

That's why you *must* use Divine—not earthly—technology to neutralize the devil and break free of ground control and earth's gravity. If you use the same technology the devil does, you cannot get off the ground. You can ignite your fuel, high praise, but if your rocket is still bolted to the hold-down arms (your hindrances), you'll just be doing a lot of shaking and rattling.

Similarly, if you put low-grade fuel in your tank (praise that includes earthly impurities), you won't get off the ground either.

In the next chapter, we'll take a closer look at the hold-down arm that was erected before the Garden of Eden incident.

Chapter 6

Humility Frees Your Rocket

The mind was created to control the body, not be an entity on its own. So whatever goes on in the mind eventually manifests in the body.

Focusing on thoughts and emotions such as courage, peacekeeping, willingness, acceptance, reason, love, joy, and peace eventually manifest as better health. Likewise, negative thoughts and emotions such as pride, anger, ungodly desire, fear, grief, apathy, guilt, and shame cause changes in body chemistry that tear down your body. The negative (lower) emotions cause adrenalin—the fight-or-flight hormone—to be continually dripped into our bloodstream, wearing down our organs and tissues.

Now you can see why the Bible repeatedly advises us things like:

> *"Rejoice in the LORD always. Again I say, rejoice!"* (Phil. 4:4).
> *"Be of good cheer"* (Mt. 9:2,22, 14:27; Mk. 6:50, 10:29; Lk. 8:48; Jn. 16:33; Acts 23:11).

"The greatest of these is love" (1Cor. 13:13).

"Love one another" (Jn. 13:34,35, 15:12,17; Rom. 12:10, 13:8; Gal. 5:13; Eph. 4:2; 1Thes. 3:12, 4:9; Heb. 10:24; 1Pet. 1:22, 3:8, 4:8, 5:14; 1Jn. 3:11, 23, 4:1, 7, 11, 12; 2Jn. 1:5).

"My peace I leave with you, My peace I give to you" (Jn. 14:27).

"Whatever house you enter, first say, 'Peace to this house'" (Lk. 10:5).

"Bless those who curse you, do good to those who hate you" (Mt. 5:44).

"Take courage" or *"Be strong and courageous"* (Dt. 31:6-8; Josh. 1:6, 9-11; 1Chr. 28:20; 1Cor. 15:58, 16:13; Eph. 6:10; Is. 41:10-13, 54:4; Jn. 14:27; Ps. 23:1-4, 27:1, 4, 31:24, 56:3-4, 112:7; Pr. 3:5-6; Mk. 5:36; Phil. 1:28; 2Tim. 1:7).

"Do not fear" (Too many to list: This phrase appears *fifty-two* times in the New King James version!)

"Humble yourself" (2Ki. 22:19; 2Chr. 34:27; Pr. 6:3; Dan. 10:12; Jam. 4:10).

"There is therefore now no condemnation to those who are in Christ Jesus, who do not walk according to the flesh, but according to the Spirit" (Rom. 8:1).

The Lord is trying to get us out of the lower, negative emotions where disease can take root and bring us up to the higher emotions that foster a healthy mind and body.

Let's zero in on pride for a moment. Pride comes out of the ego and is thought to be at the root of anger, desire, fear, and grief. A few sneaky forms of pride are judging others, feeling like a victim, self-pity, self-centeredness, and comparing yourself to others.

The ego demands to be seen, heard, and respected because the ego is focused on itself and its needs. When we perceive that our expectations are not met, negative emotions arise. Then, where your focus goes, energy flows. The more we direct our thoughts on what we're not getting or what our ego desires, the more energy our ego has available to produce stronger negative, ego-centric emotions.

It's these negative emotions (with pride the usual ring leader) that bind and blind us, bolting us to the hold-down arm on the launch pad. Negative emotions give the devil power over us—in a sense, they energize or feed the enemy. Thus we become bound up in the spiritual realm, blinded by our invigorated ungodly desires, and we can't manifest anything for the Kingdom of God.

The opposite of pride is humility, and the Bible has a *lot* to say about it. Here is just one: *"He will beautify the humble with salvation"* (Ps. 149:4, emphasis added). Salvation in both the Hebrew and Greek sense is much more encompassing than just eternal salvation, which is what we think of in the 21st century. It encompasses healing, deliverance, protection, and safety from being molested by enemies.

Humility—combined with God's intent and high praise—collapses negative emotions and energizes positive ones. This activates the *"angels, who excel in strength, who do His word, heeding the voice of His word"* (Ps. 103:20) to free you from your negative earthly conditions, circumstances, and problems. An angel that "heeds the voice of His word" is an activated angel.

Here is the Philippians 2:5-11 passage that describes Jesus' steps down into humility and His subsequent steps up into glory. For the sake of pointing out each step, they are numbered here, with my brief explanations of His humility in parentheses:

> *Let this mind be in you which was also in Christ Jesus, who, being in the form of God:*

1ˢᵗ **step down:** *did not consider it robbery to be equal with God* (Though He was God, He took a position lower than God)

2ⁿᵈ **step down:** *but made Himself of no reputation* (He didn't try to defend His reputation)

3ʳᵈ **step down:** *taking the form of a bondservant, and* (He submitted His will to the Father's will)

4ᵗʰ **step down:** *coming in the likeness of men. And being found in appearance as a man* (God became a lowly man)

5ᵗʰ **step down:** *He humbled Himself and* (He let go of His "rights")

6ᵗʰ **step down:** *became obedient to the point of death* (He died for no guilt of His own)

7ᵗʰ **step down:** *even the death of the cross* (He died a criminal's death)

~ ~ ~ ~ ~ ~ ~

1ˢᵗ **step up:** *Therefore God also has highly exalted Him*

2ⁿᵈ **step up:** *and given Him the name which is*

above every name

3rd step up: *that at the name of Jesus every knee should bow*

4th step up: *[every knee bow] of those in heaven*

5th step up: *and [every knee bow] of those on earth*

6th step up: *and [every knee bow] of those under the earth*

7th step up: *and that every tongue should confess that Jesus Christ is Lord,*

Purpose: *to the glory of God the Father.*

Our greatest model is Jesus. Do you see the seven steps down that He took to the lowliest, most despicable position a human can be, a criminal's death on a shameful cross? Then notice how God raised him up seven steps to the glory of God the Father.

How do we humble ourselves?

"The great secret to humility is not to focus on yourself at all, but to fill your mind and heart with the glory of God revealed in the sin-conquering death and resurrection of Jesus Christ." ~Brian Hedges[x]

The world's philosophy says, "live for yourself." But God's Word says, *"die to yourself"* (Rom. 6:6; Gal. 2:20; 1Cor. 15:31). Paul reinforces this many times in his Epistles, i.e., *"I have been crucified with Christ; it is no longer I who live"* (Gal. 2:20a). And he shows us the mindset to bring victory: *"Set your mind on things above, not on things on the earth"* (Col. 3:2).

This is the secret that the prophets of old knew, the first-century apostles knew, the early church fathers knew, the desert monks knew, the leaders in the First and Second Great Awakenings knew, the revivalists of the 1800s and 1900s knew, and now you know. Each time we die to the ego, die to selfish desires, we are taking a step in humility.

It's probably accurate to say that every Christian has had some kind of battle with pride. But pride is sneaky because there are so many subtle forms of it. Any emotion you give attention to—positive or negative—you energize. So unless we're vigilant to keep the different forms of pride in check, we give them life. One big showdown with pride in your life is probably not going to immunize you from all the other forms. So be on the alert for the subtle ways pride creeps in and bolts your faith down to the earth.

It's possible that being preoccupied with a subtle form of "self" holds you down. Some call it "the 'I' syndrome." Here are some examples:

- Self-absorption (preoccupied with one's own affairs, especially to the exclusion of others)

- Self-promotion (To a group of tired moms: *"I get such great sleep because I trained my newborn to sleep all night"*)

- Self-pity (*"Why is everyone always picking on me?"*)

- Unteachability (*"I've got it all figured out"*)

- Intolerance (*"You don't believe what we believe, we're right, so you're out"*)

- Self-sufficiency (*"We'll just muddle through until we get to heaven"* or *"I won't bother God—I'll get healed when I get to heaven"*).

I believe that when you're in true unity with God, you *"have the mind of Christ"* (1Cor. 2:16), and you no longer see yourself as an individual. Jesus certainly didn't look at Himself as the earthly son of Mary.

Fortunately, the very first biohack you learned in Chapter 3, high praise, has a way of very gently freeing us from our ego when we make it part of our daily life. Our consciousness breaks free of "me, myself, and I" and we find our minds are set on *"things above, not on things on the earth"* (Col. 3:2).

I have a file folder stuffed with testimonies of healings that occurred when I prayed for myself or others. As I look over the dates, I can see a correlation between my ego rising (pride) and healing miracles reducing. The more thought and energy I gave to my ego, the fewer the miracles. The less thought I gave to "me, myself, and I," the more healings and miracles occurred through my hands.

Many years ago, a Christian friend misjudged my motive behind a comment I made and corrected me. When I earnestly told her what I was truly thinking, why I made that comment, she didn't believe me and continued to correct me.

Instead of getting hurt or offended, I took it to God with a tender heart and asked Him to please show me how my motive was wrong so I could apologize and make things right. (I don't pass every test this well!) I felt the Lord affirm to me that my motive was pure and to just pray for and bless this friend. *"But I say to you, love your enemies, bless those who curse you, do good to those who hate you, and pray for those who spitefully use you and persecute you"* (Mat. 5:44). It's hard to do that for someone who I perceived hurt me, but God gave me the grace to bless her every time I thought of her.

Within the next six months, I received three major healings through biblical biohacks and got off the last three prescription drugs I had been taking for hypothyroidism, adrenal fatigue, and a sleep disorder from narcolepsy.

My friend later reported that shortly after that incident, she had the worst sinus infection of her life and lost her sense of smell for a year. Killing your ego powers up the miracles. Giving reign to the ego dampens the anointing. It could be a coincidence, but I have noticed this happening many other times.

Here's an example when I've been on the flip side of this, too. After a vacation, my husband sent some pictures to our family and friends. One of those pictures was very unflattering of me—I looked eighty years old (this was when I weighed less than a hundred pounds and my flesh was hanging). My pride reared up and I lit into my poor husband, yammering on and on about how he could do such a thing.

While I was spouting off, I distinctly heard the Holy Spirit say, "You need to back off. You need to apologize. He didn't mean any harm." I was so indignant that I did not back off until I had given full vent to my anger.

Well…you know the saying that a prideful person is "big-headed"? Over the next few hours, my head literally swelled up. It got puffy and spongy, and I developed the worst migraine I'd ever had. Soaking my head in a sink full of ice water did nothing, so I laid on my bed with an ice pack. The pain was so excruciating that I honestly thought a bullet in my head would give me some relief by reducing the swelling. I wondered if the emergency room would pump enough morphine in me to get me out of this pain. Four hours into this, I cried to God, "I can't take it. *Please*—fix it or take me home!"

Just then, I felt a tug inside my head at the base of my brain and heard a soft pop. Then I heard something like a gentle toilet flush, the swelling drained out of my head in about thirty seconds, and the head pain stopped. I was a sweaty mess, but every stab of pain had vanished in seconds.

I had been playing in the devil's playground with pride, got caught, and Papa God swooped down and fixed the mess I'd gotten myself into. Ever since then, I confess the *second* I realize I am operating in pride.

During the time I was director of a non-denominational church prayer ministry team, we developed a reputation for operating in a healing anointing. In my experience and observation, there is so much grace when those who operated in pride responded with a soft heart when the Holy Spirit convicted them. Like the relief I got when Daddy God pulled the plug in my head, the humble person's healing or breakthrough came swiftly.

Of course, I don't know what is in everyone's heart. But I have never seen anyone get healed who willfully, stubbornly held onto their pride after the Holy Spirit pointed it out to them. We examine our hearts not to be condemned but to allow the Holy Spirit to show us how we can change to be more like Him.

Socrates said, "An unexamined life is not worth living." Repentance means to examine yourself and change the way you're thinking, to move beyond your present mindset. And *'with repentance comes times of refreshing from the presence of the Lord'* (Acts 3:19, paraphrased). To me, that is a life truly worth living.

Again, pride is not the *only* reason why everyone does not get healed. But I've personally experienced and also seen in others how pride is a *big* obstacle to seeing God's power move through us. Nursing any level of pride in the heart is like handling a cactus—it's really easy to get stuck, both physically and spiritually.

ACTIVATION: Humility Opportunity

1. **Breathe the breath of God.**
   (Chapter 4 activation, page 62)

2. **Let the Holy Spirit search you.**
   "Search me, oh God, and know my heart; test me and know my thoughts. See if there is any wicked way in me, and lead me in the way everlasting" (Ps. 139:23-24 CJB).

   "Lord, is there any form of pride that I have given energy to?" (If you don't hear anything, browse the list below to see if the Holy Spirit pricks your heart. Write down whatever comes to your mind.)

   - Is there any way that I have insisted on having my likes fulfilled?
   - My rights?
   - My way of doing things?
   - Is there any way I have been calloused toward other members of the body?
   - Have I acted in spiritual pride or superiority toward someone?
   - Have I refused to forgive someone or refuse to even start the process of forgiving them?
   - Have I been self-sufficient (independent of You)?
   - Have I been rebellious in any way?

- Have I exalted or promoted myself? (Mat. 23:12; Pr. 25:6-7, 27:2)
- Have I called attention to my accomplishments or good deeds so that others would compliment me? (Mat. 6:1-2)
- Have I justified myself or my calloused actions? (Luke 18:10-14)
- Have I been so absorbed in myself that I've denigrated or degraded myself?
- Have I taken on a mindset of neediness or being a victim?
- Have I condemned myself? (Titus 3:3-6)
- Is there anything I need to lay down at the cross of Jesus so that the same mind be in me that was in Christ Jesus? (Phi. 2:5)
- Do I have any emotional, financial, or egotistical attachments to anything?

3. **Release and Receive.**

There's no condemnation in Christ Jesus (Rom. 8:1), and He already forgave you. So just 'fess up, thank Him, praise Him, and fill up with Him. I've found the advice of the early desert fathers and monks to be very true:

> *"Join in the worship of God for a little, and turn your mind to the Lord. This desire is something you can't conquer by your own efforts."* —Anonymous monk at the monastery at Scetis.[xi])

We cannot conquer temptation on our own. But when we focus on God, our temptations leave and we receive His forgiveness.

"Father God, I release this sin of pride, _____, to You (speak out loud what the Holy Spirit shows you or anything you agreed with from the list above). *I no longer want to hold onto it. I release this way of thinking or being."*

"Thank you so much for forgiving me. Thank You for carving this hard crust out of my heart and for making my heart soft like Yours. Thank You for placing Your Word in me to live, filling me with Your grace and truth, so I can see Jesus' glory" (from John 1:14).

"Let grace and truth overflow from my belly to bring rivers of life to everyone I encounter" (from John 7:38).

"Thank you, Jesus, for shedding Your blood that wipes clean the slate of accusations against me" (from Col. 2:14). *"You are so merciful and kind!"*

4. **Infuse Christ's mind into yours.**
    Now we'll turn Philippians 2:6-11 into high praise to enable Christ's mind to be infused into our mind (Phil. 2:5). Slowly savor out loud each phrase:

"We praise You, Jesus,
though You were in the form of God,
You did not regard equality with God
as something to be exploited.
Instead, You emptied Yourself,
taking the form of a slave,
being born in human likeness.
And being found in human form,
You humbled Yourself
and became obedient to the point of death—
even a shameful death on a cross.
Therefore God also highly exalted You
and gave You the name
that is above every name,
so that at Your name, Jesus,
every knee should bend,
in heaven and on earth and under the earth,
and every tongue should confess
that You, Jesus the Christ, are Lord,
to the glory of God the Father."

Selah! Pause and think about it!

5. **Harness the spiritual energy you just built up.**
   Remember, always direct the spiritual energy you
   built up through high praise. Just like Jesus dis-
   missed the spirit of legion into the pigs, dismiss the
   form of pride that the Holy Spirit showed you. You
   have the authority—you are seated in heavenly

places with Christ. You can say something like this: *"In the name of Jesus Christ, I dismiss _____ (form of pride) and send you off. You have no authority here; you must leave now and stay away from my family and me."*

If anything was healed from this activation, be sure to add it to the Christian Biohacking Facebook group at: facebook.com/groups/christianbiohacking so your faith will be energized and others' faith will be bolstered.

We're powering up! By fully submitting to God—killing your ego and the negative earthly emotions that arise from it—you busted the bolts that previously kept you stuck on the launch pad. Stay vigilant, though. I know I sure can't let my guards down.

As another spiritual hindrance is removed and you raise your emotions by exalting God, you may begin to feel some physical changes in your body as new neurochemicals are produced in response to your newly raised emotional state. One more tweak is needed before we enter into unity, full heart-brain cohesion, with Him.

Chapter 7

True Rest in Him Heals
& Energizes

True rest in Jesus Christ greatly accelerates natural healing and a calm brain-state by triggering the "rest and relaxation" mode (parasympathetic nervous system dominance).

Jesus said we would be doing greater things than He (see John 14:12). But we absolutely cannot do these greater things when we are striving in our own power. Those are the dead works that James and the writer of the book of Hebrews mention several times. We must be at *rest* in Him. I will explain this shortly.

It's very interesting how the ancient and modern health gurus all try to attain a sense of peace and rest. Their concept of this rest is definitely of some value because it activates the parasympathetic nervous system where healing occurs. Rest, relaxation, digestion, and healing cannot occur when the sympathetic nervous system is dominating. That's why sleep, digestion, even reproductive functions are often disrupted when we give our energy to anxieties and worries by focusing our thoughts on them.

If unbelievers can reach a restful and healing mode just by activating the parasympathetic nervous system, there is so much *more* available to the believer who activates the parasympathetic system and also enters into *spiritual* rest through belief in the finished work of Jesus Christ.

> *"[The righteous] shall enter into peace; they shall* **rest** *in their* **beds**, *each one walking in his uprightness"* (Is. 57:2, emphases added).

> *"Please, let us make a small upper room on the wall; and let us put a* **bed** *for him there, and a table and a chair and a lampstand; so it will be, whenever he comes to us, he can turn in there"* (2Ki. 4:10, emphasis added).

> *"[For God may speak] in a dream, in a vision of the night, when deep sleep falls upon men, while slumbering on their* **beds**" (Job 33:15, emphasis added).

> *"Be angry, and do not sin. Meditate within your heart on your* **bed**, *and be still. Selah"* (Ps. 4:4, emphasis).

> *"When I remember You on my* **bed**, *I meditate on You in the night watches"* (Ps. 63:6, emphasis added).

*"Our **bed** is green"* (SOS. 1:16, emphasis added). Note also the color green in the Bible is a symbol of health and healing, i.e., *"He leads me to green pastures,"* Ps. 23:2).

"Our hearts will never rest, nor find salvation, until we, too, learn to walk and glory in the power of that blood." (Andrew Murray[xii])

There are over a hundred verses about "bed" in the Bible. I've just listed a few which show one meaning: a place of rest. It's very interesting that the remaining verses with "bed" depict the opposite: a place of blood, death, sickness, and intimate defilement.

The quote by Andrew Murray above cries out to me that the blood of Jesus undoes—redeems—the evil that occurred where God intended rest and pure intimacy to take place. That could be a whole book, and indeed Andrew Murray and others have devoted entire books to this subject. I highly, *highly* recommend you read and savor Murray's book.

Let's get back to God's intended purpose for the bed: rest.

*"Let the saints be joyful in glory; Let them sing aloud on their **beds**"* (Ps. 149:5, emphasis added).

So then, Psalm 149 reveals that *rest* is another key to victory.

For the New Testament believer, rest is not refraining from work on a specific day but believing that Jesus fulfilled the law and God is faithful to keep his promises.

> *"So we see that [the Israelites under Moses and Joshua] were not able to enter in [God's] rest, because of their unbelief"* (Heb. 3:19).

> *"There remains, then, a Sabbath-rest for the people of God; for anyone who enters God's rest also rests from their works [labor], just as God did from his. Let us, therefore, make every effort to enter that rest, so that no one will perish by following their example of disobedience"* (Heb. 4:9-11 NIV).

The Israelites didn't believe that God would do what He said He would do, so they gave in to fear and unbelief, striving on their own to get what they needed or wanted. It was a dismal failure.

As a culture today, we are over-stressed and in sympathetic mode for longer periods of time than are healthy. A general sense of gratitude and appreciation is an excellent starting point to reset and heal.

Modern psychologists and neuroscientists have tons of data that support how to trigger the parasympathetic mode through breathing and high emotions such as gratitude, love, etc. Best-selling author, scientist and educator Gregg Braden instructs in one of his training modules, "to the best of your ability, feel a genuine sense of caring, appreciation, gratitude, or compassion for anything or anyone."[xiii]

That's good advice just by itself. That's pretty close to something written two thousand years earlier: *"Whatever is true... noble... just... pure... lovely... of good report... any[thing] of virtue and... praiseworthy—meditate on these things"* (Phil. 4:8).

That's great to begin with general gratitude and caring. But there is a greater level of rest and healing available to the believer when we choose to be grateful and appreciative *toward God* for *His* love, caring, mercy, and compassion for us. The Apostle Paul writes that first comes the natural, then the spiritual, and the natural is of some value (1Cor. 15:46). So let's be mindful of moving on up!

For seventeen years, during my thirties and forties, I was treated with medication for ADHD. Whenever I forgot to take my meds, thoughts, concerns, and bits of information continually floated around my head and distracted me. I needed the meds to drive safely, teach in a classroom, finish tasks, etc.

One weekend I drove several hours away to my parents' home for a visit. Around midnight that Friday evening, long after my ADHD meds had worn off, I finished reading an old Christian classic, *The Power of the Blood of Jesus,* by Andrew Murray. In deep gratitude, I clutched the book to my chest and contemplated all that Jesus' blood did for me.

Suddenly, like a genie sucked into a bottle, all those thoughts and concerns that floated around my head shrunk down into nothing. At the same time, my awareness of God shifted from being *all around me* to dwelling in *the very core of my being*. My brain was suddenly in a state of calm awareness as if I had taken the best ADHD meds ever invented. It was like Paul described in Acts 17:28, *"For in Him we live and move and have our being."*

The next morning when it was time to take my meds, I realized I had forgotten to bring them. I did great all weekend. On Sunday, I drove all the way home unmedicated, maintaining perfect attention on the road. In that Jesus-moment of profound gratitude and appreciation for His perfect blood, my brain permanently changed. Once home, I tossed out the rest of the meds and have never again felt the need for them.[5]

Even though He is now truly the center of my being, and I am very aware of living and moving in Him, there are times when events or people pull me out of that peace. So my *labor* to get back into rest is to go back to that place of feeling deep gratitude and love for Him and His sacrifice.

Being grateful for anything puts you into parasympathetic mode and gives you a sense of peace and rest. But rest is so much deeper and longer-lasting when you focus your gratitude on the most powerful substance in the universe: the blood of Jesus.

True and deep rest in Him may look different for you, but it will always trigger parasympathetic dominance, which is where healing can occur. In this chapter's activation, you will learn how Andrew Murray's biblical revelation of the blood of Jesus can bring you into deep rest.

There are different definitions and ways of applying the blood of Jesus among our brothers and sisters in the church, all beautiful. The theologians have worked out

---

[5] Do not stop taking your prescription medications without your doctor's supervision. Ask your qualified medical practitioner to work with you on reducing or eliminating a prescribed medication.

the details.

In my limited observation, it seems to boil down to re-membering in some way the singular, atoning sacrifice—the greatest measure of love—that "gifts" us with peace not only with God, but within God, within ourselves, and with each other.

So in this activation we are giving our voice—putting into the atmosphere—what the Bible says about the *wonder-full* blood of Jesus.

ACTIVATION: Rest is a Biohack

Repeat out loud each of these paraphrases of scripture[xiv] on the power of the Blood of Jesus. Don't try to get through all of these in one sitting. Do this exercise slowly to savor and cherish all that Jesus did. You can find this list also in the free *Companion Workbook* at: TheHighPraise.com.

The Power of the Blood of Jesus

LIFE. *"Oh God, you teach through the writings of the Old Testament that 'the life is in the blood.' Jesus' life is in His blood"* (from Lev. 17:11).

FULFILLED MESSIAH. *"When John the Baptist announced Your coming, Jesus, he spoke of You as the promised 'Lamb of God, which takes away the sin of the world'"* (from Jn. 1:29).

OVERCOMING POWER. *"I overcome the one who accuses me by personally testifying to what the Word of God says the blood of Jesus does for me!"* (from Rev. 12:11)

ACQUITTAL. *"Thank You, God, for wiping away the record against me. You took every decree away from my midst by nailing them to the cross of Jesus the Messiah"* (from Col. 2:14).

REDEMPTION. *"Through Your blood, Jesus, we have redemption: deliverance and salvation. In You, our offenses, shortcomings and trespasses are forgiven in accordance with the riches and the generosity of Your gracious favor"* (from Eph. 1:7 AMPC).

FORGIVENESS. *"Through Your blood, Jesus, the guilt of all my sins is removed"* (from 1Jn. 1:9).

JUSTIFICATION. *"Through Your blood, Jesus, I am justified, acquitted, and found not guilty"* (from Rom. 5:9 and Is. 61:10).

SANCTIFICATION. *"With Your blood, Jesus, You sanctified me—you separated me from sin and made me perfect. You made me holy with God's holiness!"* (from Heb. 13:12 and 10:10).

ACCESS TO THE FATHER. *"Thank You, for Your blood, Jesus, which gave me confidence to enter into the presence of God"* (from Heb. 10:19).

INTERCESSION. *"Thank You, for Your blood that continually cries out for mercy to the Father in heaven on my behalf"* (from Heb. 12:24).

PROTECTION. *"Your blood, Jesus, applied to my spirit, soul and body, causes the destroying plague of death to pass over me"* (from Ex. 12:7, 13).

RESTORED RELATIONSHIP. *"Thank You so much, Jesus, for reconciling me to the Father. Your blood has given me favor and friendship with Him, and made me blameless before Him"* (from Col. 1:20, 22).

JOY. *"Thank You, God, for the joy of knowing that sin is powerless to separate me from You for even one moment. Your love and mercy are over-the-top 'My cup runneth over, and goodness and mercy will follow me all the days of my life'"* (from Ps. 23:5b, 6a).

PRAYER: *"Lord, help me to surrender my heart fully to the power of Jesus' blood."*

Selah! Pause and think about it!

If anything was healed from this activation, be sure to add it to the Christian Biohacking Facebook group to build up our faith: facebook.com/groups/christianbiohacking

We've engaged, now, with all the components mentioned in Psalm 149 at the beginning of this book. Congratulations—you've come a long way! Now you're ready to take this stack and step into high gear so you can take back some territory that the enemy stole.

Chapter 8

How to Wield the Two-Edged Sword

E ngaging in high praise while in spirit, soul, and body unity and with God and His will, sharpens both sides of the sword and activates angels to bring His life and health to your body (Heb. 4:12, Ps. 103:20). Psalm 149 indicates that there is a special way available to activate the two-edged sword.

We learned what high praise is in Chapter 3 and began to train our senses to detect God's manifested presence when He comes with His entourage to sit on the throne of your high praises. It is a good king's pleasure to bless! In this chapter, we will put together everything we have learned so far.

> *"Let the **high praises** of God be in their mouth and a **two-edged sword** in their hand"* (Ps. 149:6, emphases added).

> *"Angels are ready to "obey his word, who carry out his orders"* (Ps. 103:20 CJB).
> *"You will have what you say"* (Mark 11:23).

This is exciting: it is our *honor* to activate our fellow servants to carry out the Most High God's written judgment (Ps. 149:9). This is not available to pre-saints, non-saints, or the rest of creation.

Queen Esther needed a huge miracle. So she followed court protocol, donned her royal robes, and humbly waited in the inner court for the king to allow her to enter.

By the second night of the banquet which she prepared for the king, he was so pleased to bless her that he said, *"What is your petition, Queen Esther? It shall be granted you. And what is your request, up to half the kingdom? It shall be done!"* (Esther 7:2).

It was at this point that she made her request, which the king granted. The annihilation of the Jewish people was prevented. Following protocol got Esther her victory.

It is similar for us. We don our royal robes with five components in Psalm 149:1-6 (a new song, joy, humility, rest in Him, and high praises). This "protocol" brings our spirit, soul and body, with the heart at the gateway, or seat of the emotions, into agreement with God's revealed will. (There are other keys in verses 1-6, but they are technologies for future volumes.)
We already know that the world can reach a level of

healing just by utilizing the science portion of the bio-hacks. For example, positive emotions have been shown to improve body chemistry that promotes health and healing. We also know that chronic negative emotions such as fear and anger cause adrenalin to drip into the bloodstream and tissues, wearing down organs and tissues and causing sickness. Current data has documented tens of thousands of healings just by deliberately feeling the highest-vibrating emotions of love, kindness, peace, joy.[xv]

The unbeliever, operating from only two-thirds of the man God intended (body and soul, but no regenerated spirit). He hits a ceiling and cannot go any higher than the earthly, physical limitations, however wonderful they are (for example, getting healed of a terminal disease).

"Your Father in heaven…sends rain on the just and on the unjust" (Mat. 5:45). God created healing for unbelievers, too. But *"Elijah … prayed earnestly that it would not rain; and it did not rain on the land for three years and six months."* Believers can go beyond natural phenomena.

So then, when the believer—because God dwells in us—resonates in unity with the God of the universe and speaks His Word according to His will, there really is no limit. Right now, there are people on this earth doing the greater things Jesus said we would do. Missionaries

David Hogan and Heidi Baker have documented *hundreds* of instances of raising people from the dead, multiplied food to feed the hungry in Mexico and Mozambique, and opened scores of blind eyes and deaf ears.

In Chapter 3, I described for you how two ruptured discs in my neck spontaneously healed and popped back into place during high praise. I neither asked for the healing nor spoke the Word of God that applied to my neck. *That's* how powerful high praise is! Let me tell you what happened when I put everything together from Psalm 149.

I used to teach healing classes at a supernatural ministry school. One quarter, I started every class with a six- or seven-minute song of pure high praise and did that every week for the ten weeks of the course. [The two songs I played were *El Elyon (Most High God)*[xvi] and *Kadosh (Holy)*[xvii] both by Paul Wilbur.] When the song ended, the whole class stood in reverence and awe, basking in the super-charged atmosphere. You could hear the proverbial pin drop. Then I prayed for anyone who had a need, applying different scriptures to each need.

There were about a dozen people in the class, and the first week we had two healings. Every week thereafter, we had three healings. One student came to class with a purple, mashed, swollen, broken toe that would not fit into his shoe. The next morning, he sent me a picture of his toe with beautiful, normal-colored flesh, no swelling, no pain, and his shoe fit perfectly!

We're about ready to enjoy the full meal deal. Which double-edged sword will you activate for the angels to wield? Remember, God will be watching for the Word you speak (Jer. 1:12) to have the angels perform it (Ps. 103:20).

ACTIVATION: Double-Activate the Sword

We can apply everything we've learned about high praise to pray for any type of need, but in this book, we are learning physical healing and biohacking.

First, find a scripture you can apply to your healing need. There are many online resources that list scriptures for various needs. To give you a good start and show you how to apply them, below are some personalized scriptures you can use for healing in general and also for specific areas or issues of the body. These personalized scriptures are also in the free downloadable *Companion Workbook* at: TheHighPraise.com. Of course, see a qualified medical practitioner for serious symptoms and diseases. But pray as well!

SCRIPTURES for GENERAL HEALING:

"God's righteous people face many troubles like this _____ (symptom or disease), *but the LORD comes to our rescue each time"* (from Ps. 34:19, NLV).

"The Word of God says that He heals ALL my diseases, and that includes _____ *"* (from Ps. 103:3).

"The same Spirit that raised Christ from the dead dwells in me and is quickening my _____ (affected body part)" (from Rom. 8:11).

"Jesus bore my sins in His own body on the cross. By his stripes, I am healed of _____" (from 1 Pet. 2:24 and Is. 53:5).

"As I reverence and awe the name of the LORD of the hosts of angels, the sun of righteousness—Jesus Christ—is rising on me now with healing for _____ in His wings" (from Mal. 4:2).

"The Words of God in the midst of my heart give life and health to all my flesh, including _____" (from Prov. 4:20-22).

SCRIPTURES for SPECIFIC NEEDS:

Abdominal: *"The wisdom of the LORD and reverence for Him is health to _____, near my navel"* (from Prov. 3:7-8).

Allergy, Sinus, Colds: *"The LORD sends His hand from above to rid me and deliver me out of great waters in my head"* (from Ps. 144:7).

Arthritis: *"The LORD is strengthening my hands, knees, and every joint. Where the Spirit of the LORD* *is, there is freedom and liberty in my soul, and in every joint to move painlessly in full range of motion as God intended"* (from Is. 35:3 and 2Cor. 3:17).

Blood: *"The Lord cleanses my blood, and all my measurements of ___(cholesterol, glucose, pressure, hemoglobin, platelets, etc.)___ are in the healthy normal range"* (from Joel 3:21).

Bone, Marrow, Osteoporosis: *"The wisdom of the Lord and reverence for Him is refreshment to my bones. The Lord is guiding me continually, and satisfying my soul in drought, strengthening, moistening, and invigorating my bones"* (from Prov. 3:7-8 and Is. 58:11a).

Cancer: *"Every cell in my body that my heavenly Father has not planted shall be rooted up now"* (from Mt. 15:13).

Ears: *"It is written, the ears of the deaf—and every degree of deafness—shall be open"* (from Is. 35:5).

Eyes: *"The Lord opens the eyes of the blind—and heals every degree of blindness. My eyes are crystal clear, deep, flexible and full of life, like the pools in Heshbon near the gates of Bath Rabbim"* (from Ps. 146:8a and SOS 7:4).

Facial: *"The Lord's presence and countenance is the joy, health, and radiance of my countenance, and as I look to Him and rejoice, my face is uplifted"* (from Ps. 34:5, 42:5,11, and 89:15).

Fatigue, Weakness, Infirmities: *"Thank You, Lord, for standing with me and strengthening me"* (from 2Tim. 4:17).

Fertility: *"It is written that 'there shall be neither male nor female barren among us, because Christ bore the curse of sin for us'"* (from Dt. 7:13 and Gal. 3:13-14).

Headaches, Migraines, Pain: *"According to the original Greek interpretation, Jesus has left His physical peace with me. Therefore His peace is dispelling discomfort and pain from my head (body)"* (from Jn. 14:27).

Heart Disease: *"The Lord is the strength of each beat of my heart. He's my shield from further disease. My heart trusts in Him, and I am helped. Therefore, my heart greatly rejoices, and with my song I will praise Him"* (from Ps. 28:7).

Infections, Colds, Flu: *"I am not afraid of the perilous pestilence that walks in darkness because the Lord* delivers me from it. No plague shall come near my dwelling" (Ps. 91:3, 6, and 10).

Insomnia: *"When I lay down, I am not afraid. My sleep shall be sweet"* (from Prov. 3:24).

Kidneys: *"Thank You, God. You make the arrows of Your quiver enter my inward parts. You bless my bread and my water, and you take sickness away from my midst"* (from Lam, 3:13 and Ex. 23:25). NOTE: the word often translated "inward parts," "reins," or "loins" is the Hebrew word for both the physical kidneys and the figurative seat of desires and affection.

Mental: *"Thank You, Lord, for pulling me up from the lonely pit full of mud and mire. Thank You for setting my feet upon the Rock!"* (from Ps. 40:2).

Nerve issues: *"You, Lord, are my confidence, and you keep my foot from being caught in a snare"* (from Prov. 3:26).

Pain: *"You, Lord, heal the broken in heart and bind up my wounds"* (from Ps. 147:3). *"Thank You, Jesus, for carrying my physical and mental pain.* (from Is. 53:4. NOTE: The Hebrew word sometimes translated as "sorrows" means either physical or mental pain.)

Palsy, Strokes, Scleroses: *"You, Lord, deliver my soul from death, my eyes from tears, and my feet from falling. I walk steadily before You, Lord, in the land of the living"* (from Ps. 116:8-10).

Skin Issues Ulcers, Wounds: *"Your words, oh Lord, are health and medicine to all my flesh. My flesh is healthier than in the days of my youth"* (from Pr. 4:20 and Job 33:25).

Teeth: *"My teeth are like a flock of sheep which have come up from the washing. Each tooth has its twin, and none is missing"* (from SOS 6:6).

Tumors, Warts: *"Every cell in my body that my heavenly Father has not planted shall be rooted up now"* (Mt. 15:13).

Thyroid (hypothyroidism): *"The Lord is the light and the strength of my thyroid gland. The same Spirit that raised Christ from the dead is living in me, giving life to every cell in my thyroid. I command blood levels of all thyroid-related hormones and substances to be at their optimum levels"* (from Ps. 27:1 and Rom. 8:11).

Water Retention: *"Thank You, God, for sending Your hand from above and ridding me of the great waters in my tissue"* (from Ps. 144:7).

Once you've found and personalized some scriptures (it helps to jot them down), you're ready to start the activation. Also make some notes on what your healing looks and feels like (to form your intent).

Be sure to observe in your notebook or the *Companion Workbook* any bodily sensations you experience.

1. **Your desire:**
   What healing do you desire?

2. **The Sword:**
   What scripture(s) agree with your desire?

3. **Intent:**
   What does that healing look like? What are the results? (Be specific):

4. **Parasympathetic mode:**
   Take a few minutes to get into parasympathetic mode:

   - BREATHING: Inhale slightly slower than you have been breathing and pause. Exhale slowly and pause. Repeat for about 1-2 minutes.

   - REST: Focus on what the blood of Jesus has done for you and His finished work on the cross.

(See the activation for Chapter 5 until it gets down into your heart.)

5. **The blood of Jesus:**
   "Thank you, Jesus, for Your precious blood. I sprinkle it on myself, my entire family, all my property, and my city. The blood of Jesus cleanses us, redeems us, makes us holy with God's holiness, and makes us righteous with Jesus' righteousness."

6. **Enter His gates with thanksgiving.**
   (Ps. 100:4) You've already begun to step through the gates by expressing your gratitude for Jesu's blood. Continue to thank Him for other things He has done for you or an expression such as this:

   "Thank You *for forgiving all our iniquities, healing all our diseases, redeeming our lives from destruction and crowning us with over-the-top loving kindness and tender mercies. You satisfy us with good things so that our youth is renewed like the eagles"* (from Ps. 103:3-5).

7. **High praise:**
   Read out loud and savor some of these paraphrased scriptures below regarding what God says about Himself—how He wants to be praised so He can fill you with Himself (Ps. 22:3, *"You are holy, enthroned*

on the praises of Israel"). Relish each scriptural revelation about the character and nature of God. You don't need to get through all of them. Just ask the Holy Spirit to point out a few for you to savor right now.

So that we can get a tiny handle on God's indescribably immense, unending, and flowing nature, I've attempted to sort the high praises below into categories that our finite brains can focus on.

High Praise for...

God's Power. *"How awesome You are in Your works! So great is Your power that Your enemies cringe before You. Through the greatness of Your power Your enemies will submit to You!"* (from Ps. 66:1-3).

God's Glory. *"Jesus, You are the brightness of God's glory and the express image of His person. All things are from You. All things are through You. And all things are to You. To You be the glory forever and ever. Praise and glory, wisdom and thanks, honor and power and mighty strength be to our God forever and ever. Amen!"* (from Heb. 1:3a; Rom. 11:36; Rev. 7:12).

His Rulership. *"You, Lord, have established Your throne in heaven, and Your kingdom rules over all. After You purged our sins by making Yourself purification for them, You sat at the right hand—in power and strength—of the majesty on high"* (from Ps. 103:19; Heb. 1:3c; Ps. 45:6).

His Creative Nature. *"Jesus, you are the Alpha and the Omega, the Beginning and the End. All the worlds were made through You, and you are the appointed heir of all things. You are the Almighty, the one who is, who was, and who is to come"* (from Rev. 1:8; Heb. 1:2).

God's Wisdom & Ways. *"You have made the earth by Your power, You have established the world by Your wisdom, and by Your understanding You have stretched out the heavens"* (from Jer. 10:12).

His Tremendous Love & Mercy. *"Your Love, oh God, is so wide, so long, so deep, and so high. As high as the heavens are above the earth, so great is Your mercy toward those who fear You. As far as the east is from the west is how far You have removed our transgressions, rebellions, and sins from us"* (from Eph. 3:19; Ps. 103:11,12).

God's Holiness. *"You are holy, holy, holy, LORD God of hosts! The whole earth is full of Your glory!"* (from) *You are high and lifted up, and You inhabit* *eternity. Even Your name is Holy. There is none holy like You, LORD, and none besides You"* (from Is. 57:15; Is. 6:3; 1 Sam. 2:2a).

His Faithfulness. *"Oh LORD God of hosts, who is mighty like You, Oh LORD? Your faithfulness in ful-filling Your promises, Your fidelity, Your steadfastness, and Your steadiness is round about You—it's just part of who You are"* (from Ps. 89:8).

8. **Hold Your Intent in your Heart:**
   Like a mother broods over her baby. The Holy Spirit did this in Genesis 1 when God created the world.

9. **The Two-edged Sword:**
   As you stay in rest in Him and in awareness of Who is in you. Now speak the Word of God that you personalized or selected above.

10. **Thank Him in faith:**
    The highest expression of faith is to thank God for the miracle before you see it. Your goal is to stay in rest and thanksgiving for ten minutes. But just start with one minute, then stretch it to two minutes the next time, etc. Here's how I extend this feeling, giving more time for my body chemistry to change:

    a) *Smile with your eyes.*
    b) *Smile with your mouth.*

c) *Gently touch the center of your chest—right over your heart—and "smile" with your heart.*

d) *Continue that feeling of gratitude and joy for the answer that's on its way. You framed it with your intent and the Word, and now angels are in the eternal realm performing it. It's only a matter of time before it manifests in this realm. Keep intentionally feeling gratitude and joy while lightly touching your heart.*

If anything was healed from this activation, be sure to add it to Christian Biohacking Facebook group so your faith will be energized even more, and others' faith will be strengthened: facebook.com/groups/christianbiohacking

Soaking in the atmosphere of heaven is fabulous and very healing to the soul, which often spontaneously triggers the body to heal. But making a habit of only soaking can make us spiritually lazy and stunt our spiritual growth. High praise with loving intent and the Word is a spiritual technology that God gave us to advance His kingdom on earth and bring changes into our lives.

As mature sons of God, it's our honor to wreak havoc with God's enemies (Ps. 149:7-9). Psalm 149:3 gives us more biohacking technology that is just now exploding in the science world. Yet it's been in the Bible since the very first chapter of Genesis.

Chapter 9

Sound & Frequency

S ound and frequency are powerful healing forces. They are even more powerful when a believer combines this God-created force with rest in Him, humility, high praise and joy! Again, joy and peace are high emotions that the Bible exhorts us to foster. And modern science shows how just those two emotions can heal the body. The believer has humility before God and high praise in addition to the positive emotions that the world can focus on. Now add sound and frequency as Psalm 149 refers to (we'll look at those in just a moment) and you have a *lot* of force there!

Don't panic. I want to reassure you that this is not New Age stuff; it's just science. Everything in the universe vibrates, and there are different ways of measuring how often—how frequently--one vibration cycle is completed. That is all frequency is.

We can hear a range of frequencies from 30 to 20,000 Hertz, or vibration cycles per second. The human voice range is smaller, from about 80-260 Hertz, which is somewhere around the second "E" you see on a piano to the fifth "G." Dogs can hear higher frequencies, and cats even higher. Ultrasound is out of our hearing range and varies from about 50,000–2 million Hertz.

So back to the Bible and Psalm 149. We inhabit a world that is frequency-created (*"In the beginning...God said..."* Genesis 1). And this world is frequency-sustained (*"[He is] upholding all things by the **word** of his power"* Heb. 1:3). His powerful Word is still holding everything together.

Because of the inherent power of certain frequencies, New Agers have picked up on it and added their own labels and explanations of why it works. But the use of frequencies to heal is something we should not ignore! Since God created the world with sound, which comes in frequencies, and He's in us and we're in Him, we can consciously take back God's creative and restorative powers of sound. Look at these keys to victory:

> *"Let them [**intensely**] **praise** His name with the **dance**...**sing** praises...with **timbrel** and **harp**"* (Ps. 149:3, emphases added).

> *"Let the high praises of God be in their **throats**"* (Ps. 149:6a CJB, emphasis added).

> *"Behold, the glory of the God of Israel came from the way of the east. **His voice was like the sound of many waters;** and the earth shone with His*

glory" (Ezek. 43:2, emphasis added).

*"I heard, as it were, **the voice of a great multi-tude**, as the **sound of many waters** and as the sound of **mighty thunderings**, saying, "**Alleluia! For the Lord God Omnipotent reigns!**"* (Rev. 19:6, emphases added).

This is all sound and frequency talk. In Psalm 149:3 above, the form of the verb "praise" is the intense form. One interpretation for the Hebrew word for throat in verse 6 can be interpreted as "loudly." A soft praise would be on your lips, but a loud praise must be projected from the throat. However, that Hebrew word for "throats" indicates something deep, maybe a low tone, perhaps an unutterable groan.

The uses of sound and frequency are repeatedly demonstrated in the Bible, recorded in other ancient texts, and still practiced today.

The prophet Ezekiel tells us that God's voice is like the sound of many waters. And in the book of Revelation, Apostle John describes that when God's people united in praise, it sounded like many waters.

Even if you don't have another human to lift up God's name with you, when your spirit, soul, and body are in unity, then you remove the hindrances to fully uniting with the Many Waters (Jesus) living in you, and your voice becomes a mighty thundering in the spiritual realm.

There was an interesting study published in the *Journal of Strength and Conditioning Research* in 2014 that measured the increase in athletic power from grunting, another way of vibrating. *"The velocity, force, and peak muscle activity during tennis serves and forehand strokes are significantly enhanced when athletes are allowed to grunt."*[xviii] No wonder my mother grunted when she picked up something off the floor—it helps! She got a little extra "oomph" to come back up.

The current body of scientific data that supports the ability of sound and vibration to resolve many health issues and rewire the brain is virtually exploding.[xix] It's well-established that a sick organ, tissue, or body vibrates at a lower frequency than a healthy one. The emerging science is still figuring out efficient modalities to raise the sick or diseased part to healthy vibrations. Bioacoustics, neuroacoustics, law of resonance, binaural & isochronic beats, vocal profiling, and neuro-linguistic programming are some of the new modalities and technologies that are still in their infancy.

> "We're especially and powerfully connected to and responsive to sound. And we don't just experience sound through our ears. We

experience it through our skin. We're mostly water, and sound travels through water four to five times faster than it does through air."[xx]

It's not the scope of this book to detail the science behind frequencies. However, if you want to learn more about this fascinating and huge subject, see this chapter's endnotes for some good resources to get you started.[xxi]

I'd been playing around with different frequencies of sound for more than six years. I have a simple NCH software tone generating app on my computer and had left it a certain frequency in the upper 200 Hertz (vibrations per second). One week while attending an online Christian meditation class,[xxii] my instructor had us hum as part of our meditating prayer. Since my tone generator was already set at a frequency that I could hum, I flipped it on and hummed with that pitch. In less than a minute, I felt flutters and buzzing in my gallbladder. (For four decades, I experienced pressure, stones, and attacks that were temporarily relieved with natural flushes. As a result, I am acutely aware of where my gall bladder is.)

After a total of maybe fifteen minutes of humming over the next two days, the buzzing stopped and my gall bladder became quiet. I wondered if the stones dissolved or if the gall bladder was entirely healed. Over the next five months, I challenged it with the usual triggers: a heavy, fatty meal and water fasting. Nothing! I haven't heard one peep from my gallbladder. Only time will tell if it was permanently healed or will need a tune-up with another ten-minute prayer-humming session.

Humming is just another way to vibrate. And since it comes out of the nose rather than the larynx and nose as when singing, it greatly increases the nitric oxide produced in the nasal passages.[xxiii] Nitric oxide helps keep blood vessels healthy by dilating them at the right times and regulates blood pressure. It also plays a role in reducing inflammation and in nerve transmission.

So the ancient eastern meditators stumbled on a great, God-given thing when they discovered that humming improved their health. Why should we shy away from what God created for everyone?

A Note About Movement.

Movement along with sound is powerful. Psalm 149:3, Psalm 145:21, Genesis 38:12, and more scriptures show the body as a tool for praising God. I'm still exploring it and experimenting with it, so I'm not yet ready to teach it. Perhaps I will in a future Christian Biohacking volume. But if the Holy Spirit moves you to move in any of these activations, go for it!

A word of caution: Music is powerful—be careful what

you listen to! Don't let the ego creep back in through lyrics. Prepare ahead of time a playlist of pure high praise songs to immerse yourself in God's nature and deeply integrate high praise into your soul. In Chapter 3, I list ten of these songs. If you want more, there is a list of about eighty in the *Companion Workbook.* These songs encompass many styles such as contemporary Christian, contemporary classic (the 80's and 90's), traditional hymns, Gregorian chants, and *a cappella* choirs. You can infuse your spirit, soul, and body with high praise while driving, doing yardwork, chores, sleeping, etc.

ACTIVATION: Sound and Frequency

Power time! Grab a pen and your notebook or the *Companion Workbook* and write down:

1. **Your desire:**
   What needs healing?

2. **The sword:**
   What scriptures back up your desire?

3. **Intent:**
   What does that look like? What negative aspects or emotions need to be shifted higher? (Be specific). You will lovingly hold this intent in your heart as you begin praising. When you actively hold it in your heart this way, you are "brooding" over it, like the Holy Spirit brooded (often translated "hovered" or "moved") over the formless earth when God created one thing at a time. When I was pregnant, I "brooded" over my child in a loving way, thinking about what his personality would be like, what he would look like, how I wanted to raise him, what values I would teach him. That's "brooding" in the biblical sense of the Hebrew word used in Genesis 1:2.

4. **Set your sound:**
   If the Holy Spirit leads you, play energetic, instrumental background music in a healing frequency. Anything by Christian composer John Tussey is

good, too. See this endnote:[xxiv]). You can also hum a loving, medium-low tone (somewhere between the second "C" and "F" notes you see on the piano) so that you can feel it in your chest. However, don't focus on your chest—you want to focus on your intent.

5. **Parasympathetic mode:**
Take a few minutes to get into parasympathetic mode:

- BREATHING: Inhale slightly slower than you have been breathing and pause. Exhale slowly and pause. Repeat for about 1-2 minutes.

- REST: Focus on what the blood of Jesus has done for you and His finished work on the cross. (See the activation for Chapter 5 until it gets down into your heart.)

6. **The blood of Jesus:**
"Thank you, Jesus, for Your precious blood. I sprinkle it on myself, my entire family, all my property, and my city. The blood of Jesus cleanses us, redeems us, makes us holy with God's holiness, makes us righteous with Jesus' righteousness, and makes it just-as-if-we'd never sinned."

7. **High praise.**
Get your high praise scriptures ready from the previous chapter or the free *Companion Workbook*.

These praises are straight out of scripture regarding what God says about Himself.

Stand up if you are able. You can praise God in any posture, but for reasons I won't go into here, I have found that it is more effective to stand when using the technology in Psalm 149.

Start with thanksgiving (Ps. 100:4). Slowly speak out loud some high praises, relishing what God reveals in scripture about Himself. Jot down in your workbook any bodily sensations you experience.

Feel free to sing the high praises in a low tone. Try to feel it in your whole body, especially if you are praying for the health of a particular body part. (Just don't overly focus on your body. Lovingly holding the intent in your heart while in awe of God is most important. This all gets easier with practice!)

Adding dancing (Ps. 149:3) brings your body in alignment with your will, intent, heart, soul, etc. Like math, division always reduces; agreement always adds. How much more power is available when every part of you agrees with God and His Word!

If anything was healed from this activation, be sure to add it to the Christian Biohacking Facebook group so your faith will be energized even more, and others' faith will be bolstered: facebook.com/groups/christianbio-hacking

Did you have fun with that last activation? Feel self-conscious? Notice anything change or shift? You just experienced the biblically- and scientifically-backed power of sound to heal and shift "atmospheres" and/or body tissues or chemistry. The Bible and science also show us that there's power in the opposite. Are you ready to learn a biohack on the quiet side?.

Chapter 10

Heart-Brain-God Coherence

Whenever you achieve unity between your mind, your heart, and God and His will, His overcoming love and intent freely flow, causing healing to begin.

"And may the God of peace Himself sanctify you through and through [separate you from profane things, make you pure and wholly consecrated to God]; and may your spirit and soul and body be preserved sound and complete [and found] blameless at the coming of our Lord Jesus Christ (the Messiah)" (1Thes. 5:23 AMPC).

This is a beautiful scripture that gives some insight on spirit, soul and body unity, and gives us insight into unity with God. The Greek word for "sanctify" means not only to "render as holy, separate from profane things and dedicate to God," but also "to purify internally by renewing of the soul."[6] Sin separated us from God in the first place. Being conscious of the sanctifying work of Jesus

---

[6] *The Outline of Biblical Usage* by Larry Pierce.

Christ—being made holy, dedicated to God, and renewed in soul—unites us with Him.[xxv]

In the activation for the two-edged sword (Chapter 8), we put together everything we learned up to that point. But I slipped in a little heart-brain coherence technique that I'm going to explain now.

> *"The LORD takes **pleasure** in His people"* (Ps. 149:4a, emphasis added).

He takes *pleasure* in his people. There is something very profound going on here! God is love and we see His unconditional love flowing through His people who are praising Him in the highest way possible. Let's look at what the Bible says of one result of the pleasure of God, who is love (1Jn. 4:8).

> *"Perfect love casts out fear"* (1Jn. 4:18).

> *"God has not given us a spirit of fear, but of power and of love and of a sound mind"* (2Tim. 1:7).

When we are in unity with Him, I believe we are resting in perfected love. And when we are in His perfect love, these two verses above reveal what then occurs: fear is driven out and we gain His power and a sound mind. So let's look closer at unity.

"Oh Lord, open my lips; and my mouth shall declare your praise" (Ps. 51:15, CSB).

Here we see David lining up his heart and mind—bringing them into unity, or what science describes as coherence. David set his desire to praise God (that's in his mind) and asked God to help his heart, the result being his mouth declaring God's praise. I think David knew what Jesus reiterated a thousand years later:

"Out of the abundance of the heart his mouth speaks" (Luke 6:45).

David knew his heart needed to line up with his will so that he would praise correctly. In another psalm, David even goes so far as to bring his body into unity (coherence) with his mind and heart:

"I will lift up my hands in praise to Your name" (Ps. 63:4 VOICE).

Notice the parts of the human being:

"I will" (the mind) *"lift up my hands"* (the body) *"in praise"* (the heart) *"to Your name."*

I believe scripture is indicating that praise and fellowship with the Lord is not just a mental activity. It is unity between the mind, heart, body, and God. The body also needs to be engaged—in some way—in this fellowship and union with God.

Science has developed techniques to achieve unity between the heart (the seat of emotions) and the brain when focused on the higher emotions. And there's a very good reason why this is important. Secular practitioners Dr. Joe Dispenza, Gregg Braden, and many others have documented scores of medical healings from this kind of heart-brain coherence.[xxvi]

> "Our and others' research indicates the heart is far more than a simple pump. The heart is, in fact, a highly complex information-processing center with its own functional brain, commonly called the *heart brain*, that communicates with and influences the cranial brain via the nervous system, hormonal system and other pathways. These influences affect brain function and most of the body's major organs and play an important role in mental and emotional experience and the quality of our lives."[xxvii]

> "Coherence is the state when the heart, mind, and emotions are in energetic alignment and co-operation," said Dr. Rollin McCraty, the Director of Research for the HeartMath Institute. "It is a

state that builds resiliency."[xxviii]

There are more than two decades of solid research and data into this, so don't ignore it. My big question again is, if secular man can induce a state where they recover faster and manage stress better through heart-brain coherence, how much more healing can the believer achieve by bringing his heart and brain into coherence with the Spirit of the God of the Universe?

I've only just begun to explore and understand this. What I've learned so far in the biographies and writings of the lives of the saints over the last two millennia is that heart-brain coherence with God—especially during communion—is what initiated many of the miracles and healings that are documented in volumes of books written on the lives of the saints.

For example, Saint Teresa of Avila is one of my favorite saints. She was a Spanish nun who lived in the 1500s and is considered one of the spiritual giants of the church. In 1970 she was given the title Doctor of the Roman Catholic Church for her prolific writing and teaching on prayer. She wrote many spiritual classics and much has been written about her. St. Teresa practiced daily deep meditation with the Lord and the Word, and many healings and miracles were documented to flow from this state of meditation with God.

It's difficult to describe spiritual phenomena with natural language. But we can take God's Word, the witnesses of the lives of the saints, and the scientific data we have and get an idea of what is happening spiritually.

I'm convinced that when the heart and brain are in coherence and focused only on God and His love, this is the moment where you slip into the spiritual realm where there is true worship in spirit and in truth. It's here that the give-and-take intimacy with the God of the Universe occurs. As you take pleasure in Him, He takes pleasure in you, which registers in you as high-frequency emotions such as love, joy, or peace.

Like two pendulums placed near each other, your body increases its frequency to resonate with the high emotion you accessed through true worship. When you stay in this coherence long enough, that part of your body which was ailing or diseased begins to vibrate faster and regains health (Ps. 149:4a).

Why don't we see much of this today in the general church? Why did the scientists have to discover, document, and describe it before the church at large rediscovered it? I propose that what we discussed earlier, the ego—pride, me-myself-and-I—is one of the greatest obstacles to the church advancing the Kingdom of Heaven on earth. God will not occupy the heart space we make for the ego or any other idol, and therefore unity with Him cannot occur to any great degree.

> "*I* have been crucified with Christ; it is no longer *I* who live, but Christ lives in me" (Gal. 2:20a, emphases added).

In order to let Christ live in us, we have to let go of that ego, the "me, myself, and I," which was crucified the moment we accepted Christ. I don't know about you, but my ego keeps trying to resurrect itself and reestablish itself in me. That's why I try to stay on guard to keep it dead. Living a lifestyle of high praise has a way of keeping that old guy down.

Here's a personal example of the healing power of what I call "heart-brain-God coherence." I went to my doctor because I'd been having a lot of digestive problems and pain. He found a mass in my abdomen about the size of a tennis ball and immediately sent me to a specialist. He said it felt "tissue-y like cancer" rather than scar tissue from all the surgeries I had in the past.
By that time, I had experienced many healings, so I went right to the Bible. Three scriptures jumped out at me:

> "There is no **fear** in **love**; but perfect **love** casts out **fear**, because **fear** involves **torment**. But he who **fears** has not been made perfect in **love**" (1Jn. 4:18, emphases added).

*"For **God** has not given us a spirit of **fear**, but of **power** and of **love** and of a **sound mind**"* (2Tim. 1:7, emphases added).

*"**God** is **love**"* (1Jn. 4:8, emphases added).

Notice the contrast between fear and love. Additionally, Paul's letter to Timothy associates the mind with love (heart) and power (God). This is an invitation to come into heart-brain-God coherence. I didn't have a name for it at the time, but all I did was cooperate with what I saw in scripture, first by making the decision (mind) to dump all my fears and fully trust God. I also had the elders of the church pray and anoint me with oil, as we are instructed to do in James 5:14. Then I just went into heart-brain-God coherence, thanking and praising Him for delivering me from yet another life-threatening diagnosis.

The clinicians put me through all their tests while every symptom quietly went away. Eight weeks later, the doctors' tests showed that not only did the original mass disappear, but three other preexisting problems in my gut had also healed! They gave me a clean bill of health with the medical documentation to prove it.

ACTIVATION: Heart-Brain-God Coherence

God is also in the still and small voice (1Kings 19:12).

This activation is very quiet.

At first, it may be a little tricky to focus this way. But with practice, you will soon be good at it, and you'll be able to do this activation often during your day.

1. **Your desire** (brain):
   What needs healing?

2. **Intent** (heart):
   What will that healing look like? What negative aspects or emotions need to be shifted higher? (Be specific):

3. **Parasympathetic mode:**
   Take a few minutes to get into parasympathetic mode:

   - BREATHING: Inhale slightly slower than you have been breathing and pause. Exhale slowly and pause. Repeat for about 1-2 minutes.

   - REST: Focus on what the blood of Jesus has done for you and His finished work on the cross. (See the activation for Chapter 5 until it gets down into your heart.)

4. **Consciously connect heart and brain.**

Touch your sternum, right over your heart, with a couple of fingers. Physically touching your heart area consciously connects the thought that is active in your mind (desire) with the intents of your heart.

5. **Consciously connect with God.**
   "Set your mind on things above" (Col. 3:2a). Just a short high praise will bring Him into this very special, conscious connection. Here is an example: *"Father, You are the perfection of beauty, and You shine in glorious radiance"* (from Ps. 50:2).

6. *Selah!* **Pause and think about this.**
   Keeping your fingers lightly on your sternum, stay in this union and enjoy Him! While holding your intent in your heart, enjoy His love for you, His pleasure in you. Love on Him. Now bring your intent for specific healing into this loving union. Feel the emotion you would feel if it was already healed or perfected.

7. **Train yourself to do this for longer times.**
   Stay there for five, seven, ten minutes (stretch yourself each time). If your mind wanders, just bring it back—no condemnation! Repeat your awe for Him. Keep a finger or two on your sternum and keep generating that emotion of joy or love or gratitude Smiling with your eyes and then your mouth helps to extend this emotion by keeping your body in coherence with your heart and mind.

8. Thanksgiving.

Thank God for His healing and praise Him for working His mighty power in you.

Some observations of this process:

- It can be difficult at first to sustain this for longer than a couple of minutes. But in time, you will develop the ability to stay in this special union for longer and longer periods of time.

- Healing can take place in a different order than you expect. It often progresses from head to toe, as in embryological development.

- I've noticed that the issues that have been there the shortest amount of time tend to get healed first, and those that have been there the longest tend to take longer to heal.

- There can be a lot of stuff in the spiritual realm that has to be taken care of in order to see healing in the physical realm. Just relax and let the Holy Spirit and the angels do their complete work. I love instant healings, but sometimes healing is a process, and I learn a lot as healing manifests.

If anything was healed from this activation, be sure to add it to the Christian Biohacking Facebook group so your faith will be energized even more, and others' faith will be raised, too. facebook.com/groups/christianbiohacking

Wow—that was awesome! You did great. Even if you achieved heart-mind-God coherence for just one minute, that was fabulous! Just build from there—it's a learning process. If you practice this every day, in about three weeks, you will begin to notice your brain is rewiring into a pattern that can easily sustain longer periods of focus. A wonderful "side effect" is that you can better focus on other things you do throughout your day.

Conclusion

I n this volume, you learned how to access the robust life God desires for you. You probably got released from some of the nagging health issues that have bogged you down. Continue biohacking every physical issue until you reach the high level of health and strength that will enable you to fulfill God's plan for your life.

Quite a few modern data-supported biohacking techniques in use today have been in the Bible all along, and many ancient cultures knew these techniques, as well: meditation, breathing, sound, certain movements, heart-brain coherence, high emotions such as joy and gratitude, intention, focus, and parasympathetic nervous system activation (called "rest" in the Bible).

For the believer, there are even more biohacking techniques available from the Bible. When these biblical techniques are combined with natural biohacks, they result in amplified and/or faster healing. As we have seen through this deep dive into Psalm 149, high praise, humility, surrender to God, rest in the finished work of Jesus' death on the cross and resurrection, and the two-edged sword of the Word of God are technologies that multiply each other exponentially.

This book has shown you how to combine these biblical techniques with ancient tradition and modern science to overcome the detrimental effects of modern life, so you can achieve vibrant health.

Congratulations! You committed to this and you practiced the different biohacks. Soon these biohacks will be flowing, flexible and become second nature. You are well on your way to advancing the Kingdom of God into the sphere of influence God has given you on this earth, starting with your own body and health.

If what you're doing isn't working, then it's time for a course correction. Paul urged, *"Imitate me, just as I also imitate Christ"* (1Cor. 11:1). Carefully choose who you will imitate.

Commit to a season of renewing your mind with the high praises of God. Do whatever it takes to get them deep down inside you, so they become a new supernatural lifestyle for you. If you do these activations several times or more a week, they will become part of you. Soon you will enjoy:

- Healing and health
- Renewed youth
- Greater energy
- More stamina
- Fewer prescription medications

Conclusion

As soon as you put this book down, grab your notebook and—if you haven't already—spend a few minutes with the Lord to ask him what He wants to heal next. He is more anxious than you to see you engage the Kingdom of Heaven to make your life, and your family's and friends' lives better.

> *"For [even the whole] creation (all nature) waits expectantly and longs earnestly for God's sons to be made known [waits for the revealing, the disclosing of their sonship]"* (Rom. 8:19, AMPC).

Creation is waiting for *you*—not the famous anointed man or woman of the hour—to manifest Jesus. So pick your next biohack and start manifesting!

You can do this—it's straightforward, biblical, supernatural, *and* cutting-edge science. It's for everyone who believes that we get to begin enjoying our inheritance this side of eternity and that God's Word works like He says it does.

Learn from my failures. Don't wait like I did and hit a lift-threatening health crisis before you turn to the Lord's technology. Don't pray like I used to for the right doctor and do nothing more. Notice now what hasn't worked in the past, ask why, and learn from your failures, too.

The doctors had to tell me I had the bones and intestines of a seventy-year-old and the eyes and liver of an eighty-year-old before I grew desperate enough to try a different way.

But once I lined up with God's program, I discovered how God wants us to partner with Him to get the physical victories we need. While learning how to use the keys in Psalm 149, I discovered some wonderful "side effects" of God's medicine:

- Greater intimacy with the Lord
- A deep, unshakeable peace and faith
- Free-flowing creativity
- Feeling much younger and stronger than my years

Just the high praise alone will lift your facial muscles and make you look radiant! People regularly tell me I look much younger than my age.

The high praise technology in Psalm 149 can be applied to many situations in your life. In this book, I have shown you how to use Psalm 149 to biohack your body so that you can enjoy robust health.

This technology can also be applied to many other challenges in life:

- Food issues
- Addictions
- Fasting
- Finances
- Relationships
- Praying for lost loved ones
- Group prayer for one individual or your city and region
- Personal worship
- Corporate worship

Some of these will be the subject of future books. If you would like to be notified when my next book on biohacking is released, just click "Follow the Author" on the Amazon page where my book is sold (visit author.thehighpraise.com), or join my Christian Biohacking Facebook Group: facebook.com/groups/christianbiohacking

I am certain there are many more biohacks in scripture just waiting to be discovered. *"It is the glory of God to conceal a matter, but the glory of kings is to search out a matter"* (Prov. 25:2). Perhaps you will discover some biblical biohacks, too!

Acknowledgments

I wish to first and foremost thank my husband, Joe. Without you and your French cooking, this book would never have been written. Thank you for handling everything at home while I ran away to the convent or hid in my office (that you vacated for me), so I could write this book. You are amazing and generous.

I also want to thank my three sons Carlos, Ian, and James, and daughter-in-love, Patricia. In your own ways, you have each encouraged me to write—and keep writing—this book. Thank you.

Thank you, Delaina Dafoe, Tricia Anderson, and Vicky Hilse, for laying down a portion of your lives to pray for and encourage me to start and finish this book, and jump over all the hurdles in between. You are all valiant, dedicated, and inspiring women of God. It is an honor to be called your friend.

Sister Leslie Lund and Sister Nancy Casale, thank you for hosting me in your Saint Teresa of Avila hermitage, for your many prayers for me to write, and the deep spiritual conversations we had when I came out of my hermitage for a writing break. If I had known you two when I was a teen and seen through you how beautiful and satisfying a deep relationship with God is, I might have become a Carmelite nun. You both inspire me to know the Lord in a richer way.

Megan Remington, your knowledge of Hebrew (and Greek and Aramaic) is mind-blowing, and your joy for the ancient languages is contagious. Thank you for setting aside the dissertation you are writing to take me into a deep dive into Psalm 149. Now finish your dissertation so I can sign up for another Learn Hebrew Academy course from "Dr. Remington."

Taylor Remington, thank you for your in-depth and fun teaching on Christian meditation, the foundations of the Church, early Christian and Jewish mysticism, the church fathers, and the early saints. I kept hearing snippets of your lectures in my head while I wrote this book. Heather Logan, Matt Young, Cindy Woods, Johnette Irving, Judy O'Leary, and Taylor Remington: I am so grateful for the time and thought you put into reading and evaluating an earlier manuscript. Your comments and suggestions were so valuable in shaping this book.

Donna Partow, your workbooks and videos on writing are thorough and astounding, and your incredible marketing expertise makes me dizzy. It is such a blessing to be mentored by you, and I will forever be indebted to you for using your super-power to get me unstuck—twice.

And to our heavenly Father, Son, and Holy Spirit: my

deepest thanks. *"Surely You have set my boundaries in delightful places, and my inheritance shines forth like the dawn"* (Psalm 16:6, my translation).

About the Author

Kathleen Hampton always wanted to heal people, so she was a pre-med student at her state university. She was offered a spot on the waiting list at the University of Washington Medical School, but they didn't get down to her name that year. Instead of reapplying the following year, she married the love of her life and completed a Master's degree.

She began teaching as a graduate teaching assistant and continued to teach at local colleges, then started a consulting business. When her husband wanted to take a job in Seattle, she sold her business to follow him with their son. Twin boys soon arrived, so she dove into homeschooling and taught elementary, middle, and high school students through a co-op.

It was during those years that Kathleen developed what her doctors could only call "a wasting disease." She grew so thin she nearly died. That was when she dumped all her old theology and clung to God's Word and some treatments she found in the scientific literature. Disease by disease, the Lord healed her until she was better than before.

Kathleen is now an ordained pastor and studies ancient biblical languages and the Hebrew context so she can better understand the Bible and heal even more people than if she had become a doctor. She is passionate about seeing people healed so they can enjoy the long, abundant life they were created for and complete the mission God has for them on earth. She and her family, including four grandchildren, live in the Pacific Northwest.

Send the Healing Forward

Thank you for choosing this book to learn how to combine biblical and modern wisdom to get healed quickly. Would you help other people find this book by sharing a quick testimony about how this book helped you get healed, transformed or blessed so they, too, can regain their health?

I would appreciate that so much.

Go to: review.TheHighPraise.com

Thank you!

Keep Up Your Momentum

It's fun to hear fresh words from the Word. But it's important to water this seed regularly so it will grow into an abundant crop, giving you a long, robust, active life. God created us to be in community so we can keep each other stirred up and pressing onward for the prize.

I have created a Christian Biohacking Facebook Group where we can connect with other like-minded believers, get more tips on biohacking, and share testimonies. Go to: Facebook.com/groups/christianbiohacking

For those who want to go deeper or need a hand getting started, I also run 5-week live, online mentoring classes. Each week I do an in-depth teaching on one biblical biohack, have a Q&A period, and then do a live activation. These classes will be announced in the Facebook Group above, but you can go directly to my website to sign up at: TheHighPraise.com.

Abundant blessings to you,
Kathleen Hampton

End Notes & Resources

Introduction
[i] stats.oecd.org/Index.aspx?ThemeTreeId=9
[ii] cdc.gov/chronicdisease/tools/infographics.htm
[iii] pewresearch.org/fact-tank/2019/01/31/are-religious-people-happier-healthier-our-new-global-study-explores-this-question/

Chapter 2
[iv] chabad.org/library/article_cdo/aid/867674/jewish/Translation.htm
[v] *A Journey Through Jewish Prayer I: Amidah,* Dr. Eli Lizorkin-Eyzenberg, Israel Bible Center.

Chapter 3
[vi] If you need to work through forgiving someone, a great resource is *Total Forgiveness*, by R.T. Kendall, 2007.

Chapter 4
[vii] *Breath: The New Science of a Lost Art*, by James Nestor, 2020.

Chapter 5
[viii] *Quantum Glory: The Science of Heaven Invading Earth*, by Phil Mason, 2010. This is fascinating Christian insight on the intersection between quantum physics and faith that will ramp up your own faith. This isn't for the faint of (science) heart, as quantum physics is quirky and difficult to understand. But Phil Mason does an excellent job for the layman who really wants to get a handle on what most secular scientists shy away from.
[ix] Accessing the Heart's Intelligence, blog.drjoedispenza.com/blog/heart/accessing-the-hearts-intelligence

Chapter 6
[x] Brian Hedges, Hit List: Taking Aim at the Seven Deadly Sins, (Cruciform Press, 2014), p. 34.
[xi] *The Desert Fathers: Sayings of the Early Christian Monks,* Translated by Benedicta Ward, Penguin Books, 2003, p. 49.

Chapter 7

[xii] *The Power of the Blood of Jesus* by Andrew Murray, 1993, p.22. I have read three different translations, and the Whitaker House translation is the easiest to understand for me. Plus, that translation is endorsed by Andrew Murray's son.

[xiii] *Human by Design*, Deepening Practices, Module 5 by Gregg Braden. I don't agree with all his conclusions, but he has some very good research and data.

[xiv] Some of these are adapted from *The Power of Proclamation* by Derek Prince. Derek Prince Ministries International, 2002. p. 110. This is a gem of a little book, and the audio MP3 of this book (only an hour long) with study notes is available through the Derek Prince Ministries website for a very small fee: derekprince.org/Store/Products/1000034554/DPM_Store/MP3/Power_of_Proclamation.aspx

Chapter 8

[xv] Both the Heart-Math Institute, heartmath.org/research/research-library/, and Dr. Joe Dispenza, D.C., PhD, drjoedispenza.com/blogs/research, have produced mountains of data that demonstrate the physical effects of emotions on the body. As occurs with most individual researchers, I haven't found a central link to all of Dr. Dispenza's research. But the blog link above describes three of his latest research projects which will soon be or have recently been published.

[xvi] I like this Paul Wilbur YouTube version with beautiful slides and lyrics: youtube.com/watch?v=-3i9j-GpMco

[xvii] This is my favorite Paul Wilbur YouTube with lyrics and translation: youtube.com/watch?v=MsiLjfZoHLo

Chapter 9

[xviii] NCBI, The effects of "grunting" on serve and forehand velocity in collegiate tennis players. pubmed.ncbi.nlm.nih.gov/25412161/

[xix] Here is just one example: *The effect of low-frequency sound stimulation on patients with fibromyalgia: A clinical study*, Pain Research and Management, 2015 Jan-Feb; 20(1): e21-e27. ncbi.nlm.nih.gov/pmc/articles/PMC4325896/

[xx] Sound therapy practitioner Eileen McKusick, speaking about our human biofield and how we can influence it through vibrations and the power of sound at the Body Electric 2.0 Summit by HealthMeans.com, 2021

[xxi] *The Sound of Healing: Unveiling the Phenomena of Wholetones,*

by Michael Tyrell, 2015. This is a good layman's explanation of healing frequencies and a great place to start. He does mention his own healing tones instrumental music in healing tones in the book, but his music is inspired and awesome, and I highly recommend it. Here is a link where you can hear samples of the different types of music he has produced: home.wholetones.com/samples/. Michael Tyrell is a former Grammy-winning rock musician turned Christian, youth pastor, worship leader, etc. I enjoy his weekly "Wholetonian" newsletter that is not too long and full of godly insight and scriptural encouragement.

[xxii] Rooakh Christian meditation course, instructed by Taylor Remington. rooakh.com/meditationpracticum

[xxiii] Humming greatly increases nasal nitric oxide, pubmed.ncbi.nlm.nih.gov/12119224/, accessed 05-14-2021.

[xxiv] I highly recommend anything by John Tussey. He produces outstanding and beautiful music in many different healing frequencies. johntussey.com

Chapter 10

[xxv] For those of you who want to go deeper into union with God: Many of the early church fathers and saints pursued this union. Though spiritual experience is difficult to write about, you can find scattered in the their volumes of biographies and autobiographies can be found golden nuggets of insight to how they attained this beautiful union with God. Sr. Leslie Lund, author of *Journey into Divine Intimacy with St. Teresa of Avila,* Carmelite Sisters of Mary

Publishers, 2019, has just published an excellent, very understandable study and meditation guide to St. Teresa of Avila's masterpiece on prayer and the spiritual journey, *The Interior Castle.*

[xxvi] See descriptions of Dr. Joe Dispenza's three recent studies (soon to be published) in Chapter 9's Endnote above. Here is a page that links you to Gregg Braden's research and NY Times best-selling books. He is definitely secular, but he pokes in *every* corner, including scripture to link "the Field that Connects all Things" with this physical world. greggbraden.com/additional-resources/

[xxvii] *Science of the Heart,* Introduction. heartmath.org/research/science-of-the-heart/ (This links you to the free eBook download.)

[xxviii] heartmath.org/articles-of-the-heart/the-math-of-heartmath/coherence/

Printed in Great Britain
by Amazon

13165597R00106